How Shall I Live?

A Field Guide to an Examined Life

HOW SHALL I LIVE?

A FIELD GUIDE TO AN EXAMINED LIFE

Peter Sheldrake

Travelling North

How Shall I Live? Copyright © Peter Sheldrake

All rights reserved. Except as permitted under the US Copyright Act of 1976, no part of this publication may be reproduced, distributed, or transmitted in any form or by any means, or stored in a database or retrieval system, without the prior permission of the publisher.
Travelling North
4496 Cotswold Road
Pfafftown, NC, 27040
www.travellingnorth.com

ISBN Number: 978-0-578-10493-5

This work is licensed under the Creative Commons Attribution-ShareAlike 3.0 Unported License.
To view a copy of this license, visit
http://creativecommons.org/licenses/by-nc/2.5/
or send a letter to:
Creative Commons
171 Second Street, Suite 300
San Francisco, California 94105 USA

To Linda

Preface

When I was at school, I was the proud possessor of A Field Guide to the Birds of Britain and Europe – a book I still possess. It was a comprehensive guide, listing the habitat, appearance, flight characteristics, songs and distribution of some 453 birds. At the front there was a summary listing all those bird species, which you could check off as you saw them. Hard to recollect now, but I can still see myself, as a teenager, enthusiastically lying on my stomach on the edge of Staines Reservoir, close to London Airport, looking through binoculars at what to most people would seem to be an undistinguished and uninteresting wader. There it was, a Yellowshank (nowadays called a Lesser Yellowlegs)! Another bird ticked off on my all time list!

In other words, I was a collector. I collected birds I had seen. And railway engine numbers. Aircraft registrations. Car registrations in order from 1 to 999. Postage stamps. Eagle comics. By the time I was an adult living in Australia, I was still a collector: my big thing for a number of years was every Australian Penguin Book title, from AU1 onwards. Like many a collector, I gained my satisfaction from the act of collecting itself. It was only much later that I started to re-examine that process, and to look at what I was collecting – to read all those books I had acquired, to learn more about those birds on my list.

Now I see a field guide in a different light. It is no more than it says – a source of advice to accompany you as you travel, providing a series of criteria to assist you to see things more clearly. In a complex world, we need field guides to help us traverse some very difficult territory. Some guidance is given to us at school – through learning the skills of mathematical reasoning, reading, critical thinking and project planning. Other sources of guidance are more deeply embedded in our culture, as with the foundational texts of various religions that give us the basis for developing ethical, caring and responsible relationships with others. Yet another source of assistance comes from philosophers, who have always been interested in how we should live. As experts in their field, many philosophers can become very specialised, and their ideas close to impenetrable, but nevertheless the general precepts and frameworks they offer can be a further source of assistance in making our way through the world.

One philosopher whose comments have always been a provocative source of questions and ideas is Socrates (or to be precise Socrates as relayed to us through Plato's dialogues). In the Apology as he is being tried for his life, Socrates is said to have commented; "an unexamined life is [a life] not worth living". Perhaps one of his most famous aphorisms, it is the basis of this book. As a field guide to living an examined life this is a book to help you think about your life, and consider what you might want to do differently in the future. Like a good field guide, it does not provide answers, but just gives you tools to identify and examine what is important: only you can determine the answers that make sense for you and your circumstances. Unlike my bird book, it is not a 'spotter's guide': there are no distinctive types of plumage or song to seek out. It does not tell you what decisions you should make, but rather it is a 'questioner's guide', asking you to explore issues to do with making choices about such subjects as loyalty, artistic creativity, wisdom and knowledge, managing your time, and determining how to live with others.

So, why did I decide to write a field guide? I was sitting in a bookshop one July, listening to William Powers talking about his new book Hamlet's Blackberry. There were a number of things that struck me as he talked about the importance of being 'disconnected' some of the time, an approach he argued was a necessary response to the pervasive connectedness of digital life.

First, the underlying theme of his analysis was that we need to strike a balance, a balance between the opportunities created by new technologies – from writing through to the Internet and the iPhone – and the importance of ensuring we do not lose what we have been able to do in the past. I had started to think about the topic of striking a balance in thinking about your life some twenty years earlier, when I took part in an "Executive Seminar' conducted by The Aspen Institute. The child of two remarkable people – Walter Paepcke, a businessman and philanthropist, and Mortimer Adler, famous for his 'fat man's' introduction to philosophy – The Aspen Institute established programs to introduce participants to the ideas of great thinkers, through reading and moderated discussion of extracts from the so-called 'Great Works'. In that seminar I read a discussion by James O'Toole of what he called the Four Poles of the Good Society. That paper, which later became the core of his book The Executive's Compass, introduced me to the idea of seeing critical issues as often in tension with one another – individualism in opposition to community, for example – with the challenge being to find the right point of balance between those two extremes. The idea of find the point of balance is, in fact, a philosophical approach with a long pedigree - Aristotle was famous (among other things) for arguing in favour of the 'golden mean'.

Second, that theme of 'balance' resonated in another way. My mother was quite a demanding person, with high standards, high expectations, and a set of clear principles. I was brought up in a world where you saved for a 'rainy day', and there was an expectation that you would 'serve'. My mother demonstrated that principle by working for the local Citizen's Advice Bureau for many years after finishing her career in the public service. Above all, my mother believed in "moderation in all things", and that echoed the comments being made by William Powers. However, while moderation is about not going to extremes, it seems to me now that in some areas of your life you can only achieve what you see as being 'a life worth living' by moving to more of an extreme than is usually the case. Excessive moderation is about being stuck in the middle – uncontroversial, unlikely to cause trouble, but also unwilling to do something that matters, or pushes you against the current. I think that my mother would accept that while moderation does mean that you should be careful about being excessive, it is not a counsel for inactivity or unwillingness to take risks. Moderation is a balance against excess, but excess is often an indication as to where current limits and weaknesses apply.

How does this relate to the approach taken in this book? As you read through you will find that at the end of each chapter I have identified a criterion that I think is useful in examining how you lead your life. Each criterion turns out to be in the form of a continuum, defined by an extreme at either end, each extreme representing a very distinctive (and unlikely) way of living. Given this, I am inviting you to think about where on each criterion you see yourself today, and where you might want to be in the future. The task I am inviting you to take on is to find the point of 'balance' that makes sense to you: as you do so, I hope you will remember what I said earlier, that the point of balance is not necessarily the middle point, since to always choose the middle is to avoid making a significant commitment to an end that may be important or desirable. Indeed, in using this as a field guide, I am hoping you will assess each of these criteria, and then decide if you want to make some new choices or explore some new directions that will better suit you leading a good life as you define it, that will help you lead an "examined life".

The other thing that struck me that evening was the approach William Powers used – each of the core chapters of his book explored the situation or the comments of one person as a way to explain and develop his underlying theme. Again, that reminded me so strongly of the Aspen approach. I have been using what I learnt at Aspen for the last twenty years, in teaching, in running seminars like the one I took at Aspen, and in roundtable discussions, usually through seminars comprising moderated discussions centred on extracts from a variety of writers – not looking at their work in detail, but taking some of their key thoughts, and then seeing how they relate to everyday life. It is for this reason that I have used this approach here, and I have taken the liberty of drawing on the ideas and theories of some great writers of the past, and commentators of today. Many topics will be accompanied by extracts from some of their ideas and thoughts – and the writers from whom I will quote will range from Plato and Confucius through to Milton Friedman and John Rawls. I make no apology in using direct quotes from these writers, as they said things so well I cannot improve on their words. Moreover, while the works of the Western Tradition – and especially those of DWEMs (Dead White European Males) – have been criticised in recent years for their biases and hidden agendas, the process developed at The Aspen Institute remains helpful. As we read and try to understand and apply the ideas of others, so we extend ourselves, and more than fifty years later we no longer feel that we have to accept these writers ideas uncritically, nor do we have to pay attention solely to that literature that comprises the Western Tradition.

While that evening listening to William Powers was the specific impetus to start this book, the ideas it explores have been developed over the years, and are the results of reading, observation and discussion. Much of this book draws on those various experiences. If I learnt so much through going to The Aspen Institute, then I continued to learn through exploring the approach in the early years of the Myer Foundation's Cranlana Programme, in developing its foundational program, 'The Colloquium', itself based on the format of 'Executive Seminar'. While both The Aspen Institute and The Cranlana Programme played an important part in shaping my thinking about Socrates remark, there are many others to whom acknowledgement is due. I am particularly indebted to the members of the 'Senior Roundtable', a group of retired business and government senior executives with whom I met once a month for some eleven years, debating ideas, and trying to understand how they apply to today's concerns. I have also learnt from many of the students at my university who have been willing to debate issues outside the normally narrow confines of the MBA curriculum.

If this book draws on ideas and experiences of the past twenty years, it also has a more immediate contribution. My wife must have been stunned when I announced I was going to write a book while on our honeymoon – there can be no more isolating an experience that having a writer working away silently beside you. However, Linda played a critical role in my thinking, a test bed for ideas and a source of commentary and criticism: she also proved to be a demanding editor! She also taught me to do so many things that I had not done before. I have learnt to appreciate the visual arts, and to see so much more. I have been encouraged to think about relationships and family in ways that I had managed to skate over for a long time. She has made me examine my life more closely than ever before, and without her as a source of friendly criticism and continuing encouragement there would have been no book to be read.

I found writing this book quite a challenge – I was stretched beyond what I knew and understood to try to deal with some major philosophical issues, and I am sure this will be evident as you read through this guide. Actually, in one sense this book is about stretching yourself, past the places you have been, and exploring some territory that is new and important. In the past twenty years, I have begun to read, and begun to understand, some wonderful works of philosophy and political science, works at a level where I remain a beginner, still seeking to get a better hold on ideas and concepts. As I was writing this book, I was reading Amartya Sen's book The Idea of Justice, a deep and important analysis and one that would have been quite beyond me when I began this journey twenty years ago. However, the very fact that books like his have given me so much enjoyment, and stretched me so much is the final reason I have tried to put together something that might encourage you to do the same. Perhaps you will be motivated to read beyond this simple introduction, and spend some time wrestling with some of the major contributions made by great thinkers of the past and the present. If that is the result of your reading this book, I will be delighted.

Contents

	Introduction	xv
1.	Making Assumptions	1
2.	Ourselves and others	27
3.	Does economics make sense?	45
4.	Examining the world around us	69
5.	Reaching in to the future	93
6.	Acting strangely	117
7.	Trying to be consistent	133
8.	In control, out of control	155
9.	Opening our minds	169
10.	Now over to you	187
	Appendix: Acknowledgements and References	201

Introduction

We are curious creatures; curious about ourselves, about the people around us and about the world we live in. To ask 'why?' is part of our make-up. We watch documentaries on television, read about the lives of others, and even just listen to someone else speaking because we are driven by the impulse to find out more. That impulse to be inquisitive about everything around us seems to have been a human characteristic for a long time, and was clearly a driver in that explosion of critical thinking that took place in Greece two and half thousand years ago. Socrates was one member of a group of Greek philosophers who played a key role in the questioning, provoking and doubting of just about everything. He was driven by the concern that he was not sure that he really understood things, and therefore it was important to subject even the most simple of everyday comments to scrutiny. He did this by asking people questions about simple things such as what they meant by saying they were happy - and quickly demonstrated that these things were not simple at all! However, some saw Socrates' habit of asking questions as evidence that he was a troublemaker, even a corrupter of youth, and as a result ended up being tried for his life in his old age. In responding to questions about what he had been doing, Socrates replied, "an unexamined life is not worth living". In saying this, he was not just talking about arbitrary curiosity, but about what he saw as a necessary task, to critically assess the life we lead.

Why was Socrates so adamant that an unexamined life was not worth living? It seems to me that it is very easy for most of us just to fall into doing things, to get on with living, and never step back and ask if there is more to life than this. Socrates is asking us to take some time out and explore whether what we are doing is enough. Are we satisfied with the life we are living – not in a material sense, but in terms of feeling good about ourselves? I suppose you could say that while we have moments when we ask 'why' about something, we seldom as 'why' about ourselves. As we will explore later in this book, Socrates was concerned with more than just personal self-examination, but also the broader themes as to what we mean by justice and the nature of a good society

How can we set about the task of living an examined life? There are nine topics in this book, and each is described in terms of a continuum, defined by two extreme scenarios as to how we might live. By reading and reflecting, you are invited to examine your place on each continuum, and perhaps here you would like to be on that continuum in the future.

That must sound very abstract; so let me illustrate the approach by giving you a preview of what follows in the next chapter. As we explore how we make assumptions about other people, we are going to consider two different perspectives, seeing others as individuals and seeing others as members of a community.

When we think about others in terms of individuality, especially in today's very materialistic environment, we tend to see this expressed in terms of conspicuous - and often rather selfish - consumption, whether by getting another new television set, going on a trip to an overseas country, or just getting a good seat in the cinema. At the extreme, seeing people as individuals is to see them as focussed on themselves alone, as if the rest of the world did not really matter.

When we think about others as members of a community, on the other hand, we tend to think about peoples' willingness to give away individuality for the sake of being accepted in a group, whether this is by dress, behaviour, or even the views they hold. At the extreme, seeing people as part of a community is to see them as like clones, indistinguishable from one another.

Of course, either extreme is rather unrealistic. No one can be an individual totally isolated from the community, except, perhaps, in the case of a hermit. Equally, no one can be totally absorbed by a community, except, perhaps, in the case of some cults. These extremes mark out the extent of what we might call 'affiliation' – how we link with others. In thinking about the affiliation criterion and the continuum that runs from the extreme of isolated individuality to the extreme of the unthinking member of a community, the question to be examined is where you see yourself on this continuum. Are you closer to the individuality end of the continuum, more concerned with meeting your needs than with sharing and identifying with others, or are you closer to the community end, sacrificing your individual needs for the sake of others?

Each of the continuums is like this, providing a lens through which you can examine your life, think about what you are doing today, and consider if there are ways in which you might want to change – to move further towards one extreme or the other to be truer to the person you would like to be.

1
Making Assumptions

If you live in a modern Western country, you can see two rather contradictory activities going on around you. One the one hand, there is an enormous amount of attention being paid to people as individuals, emphasising the importance of meeting their specific needs, their tastes, their preferences. Indeed, modern technology makes it possible to talk about marketing to each individual separately – a 'market of one'! On the other hand, we can also see that people tend to congregate with others like themselves – and express their identification with others through dress, where they go and what they eat, and even how they speak. It seems as though people are both individualists and members of communities. How can we make sense of this puzzle: are people individuals at heart, or are they really members of groups, similar in what they seek?

One way of approaching this is to explore what is intrinsic to our human nature. When we deal with other people, we make a number of assumptions about them, and there are things we take for granted. Perhaps a good starting point is to acknowledge that it is important that we make assumptions about others! After all, one of the puzzles we face in dealing with people is that we can never get inside another person's head. We see everything through our own eyes, our senses, and we understand things through frameworks in our minds.

Philosophers have a lot of fun dealing with this – and have undertaken thought experiments to come up with all sorts of elaborate scenarios to consider what the world might be like – ranging from imagining there is no world outside our own head (the external world exists just in our imagination) through to contemplating a 'brain in a vat' (a brain without a body, but fed information to make it believe it was really in a person)! You might well wonder why such bizarre ideas are considered, but in both those cases, they are used to act as the basis for questioning some of our 'taken for granted' assumptions.

One part of our 'taken for granted' world has to do with similarity and difference. In thinking about the people we deal with, at one level we recognise that they are all different – in appearance, in behaviour, in preferences, in tastes. No one person seems exactly the same as another, and even identical twins turn out to behave quite differently despite the fact that they can look uncannily similar. Each person seems to be unique, and while there is a great deal of ongoing debate as to the relative influences of nature (our genetic inheritance) and nurture (the socialisation we undergo as we grow up), it is that uniqueness that makes each one of us a distinct person.

Yet, at another level, we assume that all people are the same, and have the same needs as we do for food, safety, peace, a home, and so many other things. We also assume that in some fundamental way they also have brains that work like ours, that everyone else feels emotions in the same way we do, can analyse problems, and answer challenges – perhaps coming up with different answers, but still having some common underlying mental and emotional processes. We also assume they see the same world that we see – buildings, roads, and even a beautiful sunset. That sense of all human beings sharing these same basic attributes is also what allows us to differentiate ourselves from other animal species, even though we acknowledge some similarities between the higher apes and ourselves. We can draw that distinction between ourselves and other species because we have some unique capabilities such as our ability to use language, to be dextrous, and to retain and recall vast quantities of information.

When we talk about human nature, we are referring to those attributes that we believe are common to us all. There has been a lot of speculation over many hundreds of years as to what is this thing called human nature. Perhaps some of the more interesting earlier examinations came from the Greeks. It would be nice to examine Socrates' views on human nature, but he has left us nothing in writing (indeed, he argued that the only effective way to learn is through conversation). So we have to rely on Plato, his most famous student, who wrote a series of dialogues with Socrates as the main character. There is a problem here. We cannot be certain that what Plato writes as the words of Socrates is completely accurate, as they may be Plato's views alone. However, we are not trying to resolve this issue here – and so we will treat Plato's account of Socrates' views as if they are his: we are, after all, just beginning to practice questioning!

Plato, in his famous dialogue on The Republic, presents a view of human nature that has remained central to many peoples' thoughts over the centuries. By the way, just to confuse you, most would argue that The Republic is almost certainly based on the views of Plato alone!!

Plato explores the topic of human nature in an interesting way, in a dialogue that takes place between Socrates and Glaucon – Glaucon is one of those people who appear in Plato's dialogues partly because he can always be relied upon to say 'the right thing'. On this occasion, Glaucon has taken on the role of explaining to Socrates why it is not a good idea to lead the life of a very good person, except insofar as society demands it – an interesting proposition, and one that seems, at least on face value, to be very relevant to any consideration of what might be fundamental to our human nature?

Simplifying Plato's account, it begins with Glaucon telling a story; in this case it is a story from the past about events in a Greek city-state. The central character is Gyges, a shepherd, who spends most of his time outside of the city, Lydia, looking after his sheep. Unexpectedly, an earthquake reverberates through the region. To his amazement, Gyges sees that a huge chasm has opened, which has revealed the remains of a town below the surface. He can see parts of buildings, even what appears to be a broken tomb. He can't help himself, but scrambles down into the gap to take a closer look. Inside a broken sarcophagus he sees the remains of a person, just a skeleton, with a ring still attached to one of the fingers. He pulls off the ring – and as he does so, hears some rumbling. It seems as though the earthquake is going to continue. Gyges scrambles out as fast as he can, and, sure enough, there are further convulsions. Some time later much of the scene he had been able to observe has disappeared again, engulfed in rubble and the aftermath of devastation.

Later, as the shepherds gather in the evening, Gyges is talking with his friends about the amazing events that had taken place, and while doing so, he plays with the ring in his pocket. It has a stone, with a circlet around it - a collet - and he finds the collet is loose, and twists it idly. The result is extra-ordinary. As he twists it, he becomes invisible: not just physically, but also he disappears in every other sense. Now his friends continue to talk, but they do so as if he had never been with them that evening. He twists the collet the other way - and reappears just as magically! You can imagine that he played with the ring for some time, just disappearing and reappearing.

Glaucon explains to Socrates that Gyges began to think about the power of the ring. There were so many things he could do: certainly, he could use his magical skills to acquire wealth, and become powerful and important. He goes in to the city of Lydia soon after the day of the earthquake. When he is there he uses its magic to go into the palace of the unpopular King of Lydia, seduces the queen and kills the king, replacing him on the throne.

The story of Gyges killing the King of Lydia is an old one, but Glaucon is retelling it for a purpose – and elaborating the story as he does so. Having told his story, we move on to the denouement, as it were, because Glaucon is telling this story to lead up to an interesting question.

He goes on to ask Socrates to imagine there were two such rings. One is offered to a wholly bad person, a crook and murderer shall we say, who naturally takes the ring and uses it to pursue his nefarious ends. The second is given to a wholly good person, some one who Glaucon describes as 'wholly just', who also has the ring to do with it as he wants. Glaucon continues his story, describing what happens when the *good* person has the ring:

> "No man would keep his hands off what was not his own when he could safely take what he liked out of the market, or go into houses and lie with any one at his pleasure, or kill or release from prison whom he would, and in all respects be like a God among men. Then the actions of the just would be as the actions of the unjust; they

> *would both come at last to the same point. And this we may truly affirm to be a great proof that a man is just, not willingly or because he thinks that justice is any good to him individually, but of necessity, for wherever any one thinks that he can safely be unjust, there he is unjust. For all men believe in their hearts that injustice is far more profitable to the individual than justice, and he who argues as I have been supposing, will say that they are right. If you could imagine any one obtaining this power of becoming invisible, and never doing any wrong or touching what was another's, he would be thought by the lookers-on to be a most wretched idiot, although they would praise him to one another's faces, and keep up appearances with one another from a fear that they too might suffer injustice."*
>
> (Plato, The Republic, Book 2)

Glaucon is suggesting to Socrates that everyone would use the ring, even if they were paragons of virtue! I have read this story many times with groups ranging from young students to wise, retired senior executives. Before I go on to reveal what Glaucon says in the dialogue, let me tell you what happens in those discussions. After we have read the story, I always ask the group two questions: 'Would you use the ring?' and 'Does the ring exist?'

After a little hesitation the overwhelming response to the first question is 'Yes'. The underlying theme of that positive response seems to be 'Why not?" In other words, if you have the power, why not use it. Inevitably, this leads to a discussion as to what would be the purposes for which you would use the ring. The usual path of discussion moves from exploring 'fun' uses (listening in to conversations, playing tricks), through to something more serious, (like helping the needy, or getting rid of a dictator).

However, there are usually a few (perhaps one or two out of a group of 20) who will say 'No'. They point out that use of the ring is both unfair and unsafe. Unfair, because you are able to do things which others cannot do, and therefore have an unfair advantage. Indeed, you can do things that you have no right to do – even if they are in some sense good (like that example of killing a dictator). Equally important, they point out that the ring is unsafe, in the sense that it is almost certain to be addictive: once you have used it, you are likely to use if more and more, and even if the first uses are harmless, after a while you will slip into doing things that are less positive.

In such a discussion, the topic of Lord of the Rings often comes up for discussion. The ring that Bilbo Baggins found, and that Frodo had to take back to Mount Doom in Mordor was another ring that conferred the power of disappearance. That ring was addictive: I always remember poor Bilbo couldn't help using it, even on his hundred and eleventieth birthday (to disappear at the end of his speech). At the same time, the ring was also a huge burden: the closer Frodo got to Mordor, the heavier the ring became, and the harder it was for him to even allow anyone to assist him. For those of you that have read the book, or seen the film, I am sure you can remember that the ring began to claim Frodo: in the end, he couldn't throw it into the fire on the slopes of Mount Doom, and the ring's destruction only came about because Gollum seized the ring and then toppled and fell into the fires of the mountain – eliminating both the ring and himself at the same time.

As to the second question – does the ring exist? – well, that is much easier. The ring is symbol of power, enormous power. Today, for example, those with enormous wealth hold such power – and it seems that often they can also do as they will. But if the ring is about power, then Glaucon's story of the ring is really a story about power, and how absolute power allows us to do exactly what it is in our nature to do, without any constraints.

Many writers have reminded us that those who have such power are allowed to do what they want, and do! I am fond of the Greek historian Thucydides who uses his account of what has become known as the Melian Conference (an episode in the Peloponnesian War) to present us with the succinct comment "the strong do what they can and the weak suffer what they must". Or perhaps you prefer that equally trenchant comment that "power corrupts, and absolute power corrupts absolutely"!

If we are to accept Glaucon's story, unlimited power reveals that it is in our human nature to be selfish, to do what we want: to be 'individualists' whose interests are entirely their own. Is that true? Do we 'at a pinch' always pursue our own self-interest? This was what Glaucon was arguing, and it has been a view about human nature that has persisted for a very long time. Machiavelli observed that princes and autocrats for centuries had acted in such a way – and presumed the same motivations in those they ruled (we will return to Machiavelli in Chapter 7).

Perhaps I should be more specific. Do you believe that people are inherently selfish, and will, especially when the going gets tough, pursue their own self-interest? Is this how you would view staff at work? Or members of your family? And surely – and this is the more uncomfortable part of this – if this is your view of human nature, then surely it must apply to you as well?

I was presented with an unexpected opportunity to think about my views of self-interest when I was typing this chapter. At the time, I was staying in an apartment in the old centre of a French city. During the afternoon, someone started screaming and shouting from one of the other apartments. The noise was extreme, disturbing even, and clearly something was wrong. I debated what I should do: I didn't speak French well; there was no telephone directory with emergency numbers I could call; and, in the end I resigned myself to the view that someone in the apartment block would be better able to deal with the situation (acting in the way I had done in the past in my own country). A long time later, after a very long period of screaming, there was silence, and when I looked outside first an ambulance, and then the police came.

I didn't know what happened then – nor do I to this day – but I still wonder if everything had been resolved well. Was it a psychotic episode of someone on drugs? Was it someone who had failed to take his or her medication? Should I have acted anyway? My lack of action pained me then and for some time afterwards: I kept going back to what I had not done, and questioned my weakness, my attitude, and my lack of response. I felt helpless, but perhaps I was also acting in my own self-interest, afraid of getting involved in something out of my control, where my safety might have been at risk?

That event reminded me of the much-quoted story of the woman killed in the courtyard of a block of flats in the USA. In March 1964,

Kitty Genovese returned home from work in the early morning. Despite two episodes of screaming and calling for help, an attacker raped and murdered Genovese. Only one person did call police, late in the piece, who arrived within two minutes, but by then it was too late. When witnesses were questioned as to why they did nothing, the most-common response was that they didn't want to get involved. The murderer was subsequently caught.

However, in the weeks following, coverage of the murder of Kitty Genovese took second place to the story about the witnesses' lack of help. The story has been repeated so many times as an illustration as to how we are not really altruistic, how we will not go to the help of others. However, when a journalist, Jim Rada, reviewed what had happened, he discovered that it was not the way it had been told. The number of people involved, the number of attacks, the visibility of what happened, all were incorrect, (Rada, 2009). The question this raises is, despite all this botched reporting and exaggeration, why has this story been repeated so many times? It seems it is because it confirms our belief that people are selfish, not altruistic. Is it that in some way the underlying basis of the story seems more important than the facts? Is it because it tells us something that we feel is true? We can all cite examples of people not taking action to help another – a pregnant friend of ours recently fell over in a crowded street, and no-one came to her aid. So, is it true we are selfish, not altruistic? Was I being selfish?

Certainly, we often have negative – even rather black – views of our fellow citizens. I know that on some days I seem to have a strange antipathy to people around me – not close friends, but to the general population, as it were. When I feel like that, I am reminded of Machiavelli, who once noted about men that "it may be said of men in general that they are ungrateful, voluble, dissemblers, anxious to avoid danger, and covetous of gain". I am not sure what he thought of women (although he did end his most famous book talking about fortune as if it were a woman, and said "she is always a friend to the young, because they are less cautious, fiercer, and master her with greater audacity"!!) It has to be said that neither his nor mine is exactly a very positive view, and yet it is one which, quite inexplicably, I feel from time to time (about men in general, that is!!). Is this just because I have a negative view of human nature, or is there something else here that I am unwilling to draw out of myself. And, again, if this is my view of people – at least some of the time – then surely it must apply to me as well?

In asking the question as to how we see others, and then asking if this view inevitably reflects back on how we must see ourselves, one issue is self-awareness. One way of thinking about self-awareness is the concept of 'disclosure': by this I mean, what we are willing to say about what we think (disclosure to others), and what we are aware of in terms of what we think (disclosure to ourselves).

Before we return to examining whether or not Glaucon's view of human nature is correct, it may be helpful to do a little more exploration this other facet of how we see others, and hence ourselves. There is an approach to this topic that is used in many management schools around the world, based on a model called the 'Johari Window' (Luft and Ingham, 1955).

The 'window' is really the familiar 2 x 2 figure, with two axes. One axis is about what is known by you about yourself, or not; the other axis is about what is known by others about you, or not. A typical window looks like the one shown in Figure 1:

Figure 1: The Johari Window

	Known by you	Not known by you
Known by others	A Arena	B Blind Spot
Not known by others	C Façade	D Unknown

It is common to name each of the four areas:

- A, the area where you and others know the same things about yourself, is often called the 'arena';
- C is the area where you know things about yourself but they are not known by others is called the 'façade';
- B is the area where others know things about you which you do not know is the 'blind spot'; and, finally,
- D is the area where there are things about you that are not known by you or others, is the 'unknown'.

When the Johari Window is used formally, participants choose from a list of 56 adjectives, and they are allocated to each of the four areas in the window. However, we can use it more conceptually, simply looking at the relative areas that each holds.

As you can see, the relative areas can be quite informative. In this example, the person in question knows a lot about themselves (areas A and C on the left hand side of the diagram), but chooses to keep quite a lot secret about themselves (area C – that part of the left hand side of the diagram in the lower half). They also recognise that there is a fair amount they don't know about themselves (areas B and D – to the right), and this includes some things that others do know about them if though they do not (area B – in the upper right hand corner)!

You can imagine different configurations of the window, which arise from moving the two internal lines, thereby changing the size of the various areas, and hence changing the proportions between those things known by you, those things known by others, etc. The Johari Window is not a scientific device, but an aid to thinking. It is a way of helping you think about yourself, and your relationship to others. It has been used for many years to aid managers (and others) to think about how they work with their colleagues and staff.

Going back to Glaucon's presentation, we can use the Johari window to explore the issues a bit further.

If Socrates is asking us to examine our lives, if we want to live a good life, what does this mean about disclosure – to ourselves, and to others? To begin with, it might seem a good idea to have area A as large as possible – to reduce the things we keep secret, and the increase what is know to everyone.

This is shown in figure 2.

Figure 2: The Johari Window - second version

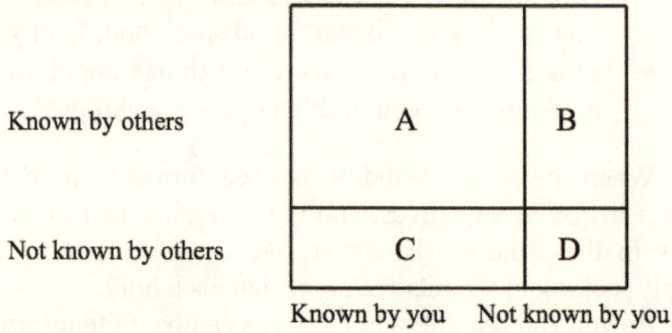

If we go back to the story of Gyges ring, Glaucon didn't stop with his statement that no one could resist the opportunity to use the ring. He was determined to make his point about the extent to which it is better to be unjust rather than just, and that people are only good because they have to be, not because it is intrinsic to their nature. In the next part of his presentation to Socrates, Gyges goes on to expand on his analysis of the just and the unjust. He argues that the best way to think about these two types of people is to consider the extremes, the 'expert' if you like in injustice and the expert in justice, each person being the perfect exponent of the art!

What does this mean? Well, let us use as an example the unjust man, the crook. If he is going to be really good at what he does, he is going to appear to be good – he will hide all his wrong doing, and to the outside world will appear to be a good, honest and upright citizen, leading a good life, contributing to society and lauded by all for being the epitome of all that a person should be! Many films and books explore this idea, the crook who appears to be the perfect gentleman, and gets all the benefits of being well regarded, while in secret doing all sorts of terrible things (it is an image we often find quite fascinating).

As Glaucon goes on to argue:

> *"Now, if we are to form a real judgment of the life of the just and unjust, we must isolate them; there is no other way; and how is the isolation to be effected? I answer: Let the unjust man be entirely unjust, and the just man entirely just; nothing is to be taken away from either of them, and both are to be perfectly furnished for the work of their respective lives... Therefore I say that in the perfectly unjust man we must assume the most perfect injustice; there is to be no deduction, but we must allow him, while doing the most unjust acts, to have acquired the greatest reputation for justice.... And at his side let us place the just man in his nobleness and simplicity, wishing, as Aeschylus says, to be and not to seem good. There must be no seeming, for if he seem to be just he will be honoured and rewarded, and then we shall not know whether he is just for the sake of justice or for the sake of honours and rewards; therefore, let him be clothed in justice only, and have no other covering; and he must be imagined in a state of life the opposite of the former. Let him be the best of men, and let him be thought the worst; then he will have been put to the proof; and we shall see whether he will be affected by the fear of infamy and its consequences. And let him continue thus to the hour of death; being just and seeming to be unjust.*
> *When both have reached the uttermost extreme, the one of justice and the other of injustice, let judgment be given which of them is the happier of the two... the just man who is thought unjust will be scourged, racked, bound –will have his eyes burnt out; and, at last, after suffering every kind of evil, he will be impaled .... [but the unjust man] .... is thought just, and therefore bears rule in the city; he can marry whom he will, and give in marriage to whom he will; also he can trade and deal where he likes, and always to his own advantage, because he has no misgivings about injustice and at every contest, whether in public or private, he gets the better of his antagonists, and gains at their expense, and is rich, and out of his gains he can benefit his friends, and harm his enemies; moreover, he can offer sacrifices, and dedicate gifts to the gods abundantly*

and magnificently, and can honour the gods or any man whom he wants to honour in a far better style than the just, and therefore he is likely to be dearer than they are to the gods. And thus, Socrates, gods and men are said to unite in making the life of the unjust better than the life of the just."

(Plato, The Republic, Book 2)

A little overstated? Well, Socrates was impressed by the work Glaucon put into his presentation, and it does seem a good illustration of the philosopher's use of stories like these – make the account bold and dramatic to draw the reader in.

In a sense, Glaucon's argument is quite simple: if you want to be really bad, then make sure that no-one realises (keep that area C in the Johari window as big as you can), and then you can be really bad and get away with it (after all there is no point being found out, as Glaucon says). However, if you want to be really good, then you must also keep your activities hidden, or else people will think you are doing all these things to be praised, to receive recognition, to be given an award (and so you, too, will keep a lot hidden – area C is very big again). For both people in Glaucon's story the Johari window will look like Figure 3.

Figure 3: The Johari Window - third version

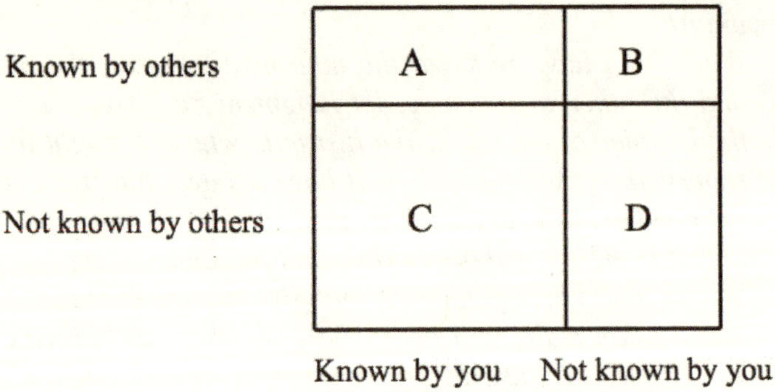

	Known by you	Not known by you
Known by others	A	B
Not known by others	C	D

Not surprisingly, the unjust man doesn't worry that people see what appears to be his good side and praises him for it (after all, that makes his real self even more satisfied, he is a crook, and praised for his good works); on the other hand, the public side of the good person must always be seen to be parsimonious, miserly, and unconcerned about others (otherwise people will think he is being good for the sake of being praised)!

Glaucon seems fairly persuasive, and in case you feel this discussion seems somewhat esoteric, remember this is a topic which causes a lot of debate today – do rich people give money to hospitals, the arts, to welfare because they are genuinely philanthropic, because they want recognition, or because they want to be seen as more philanthropic than others who are similarly wealthy? Some choose to give anonymously, and therefore are not parading their goodness. However, many others *do* want their names associated with their gifts, or the names of members of their family. The motives of donors are complex, and those seeking donations have to work hard to identify what they see as the reasons for making a donation, and ensuring those motives are satisfied.

However, to go back to the issue of disclosure about ourselves, if Glaucon is right in his argument about the perfectly good and the perfectly bad person, in either case they would want to keep their motives and their interests relatively hidden (as we have said, if they are good, they don't want to appear to be seeking recognition, and if they are bad, they don't want to be caught!). This would imply that the task of the 'examined life' is a private one, for the individual alone, not something to be disclosed to others.

To balance against that, we also believe that it is important to be part of a community, and to share with others in what we do. In the last twenty years in particular, there has been increasing attention paid to the desire to move out from the city into the country or to the coast. That attention is based, at least in part, on the assumption that many people are beginning to despair about the life of the city, where they do not know their neighbours, and live a life of virtual isolation – only connected to people at work, and a network of friends and relatives that may be located all over the world. Go back to simple living, where you are part of a small but real community, where everyone knows everyone, and there is a real sense of belonging. Oops, did I say everyone knows everyone? Together with the lack of familiar shops and megastores (as many sea-changers have discovered, there are no supermarkets just round the corner) the other surprise is that everyone knows everyone, and there are no secrets. To their horror, they realise that all their smallest peccadilloes and peculiarities are easily revealed for all to see: no secrets here!!

Be open, or be secretive? Live a life where you are part of an anonymous city, free to be who you want to be; or live a life in a community, but learn to accept that secrets and privacy are a much smaller part of your life?

As we live in a changing world, even that opposition is breaking down. The power of the internet and the systems it enables means that we can all be tracked and identified, from the responsive approach of Google to our searches through to companies using business profiling. It seems we can no longer hide in the city. Our lives and preferences are minutely examined, so that we can have the benefits of being treated as a 'market of one person', but at the same time every choice we make is noted, recorded, and used in the future. Maybe it is better in the small town – no secrets, but at least there is a sense of belonging.

If Glaucon is right, and it is in our human nature to be selfish, to pursue our own self-interest, and that we only do what is right and good because we are required to by law and the rules of society, then at heart we are individualists. Our discussion of human nature has led us to one of the most important contrasts we face as humans – between individuality and being part of the community. It would seem that emphasising what makes us different from others is about individualism; emphasising what makes us like others is about community. However, there is a paradox in this: if it is true that it is in our human nature to look after ourselves at the expense of others, then the source of our individuality is something that is the same for all of us – our self-interest!

Perhaps all this has given a rather negative view of individualism, as so far we have examined this from the viewpoint of 'human nature', looking at self-interest. There is a rather different perspective on individuality, which has to do with each person's freedom to pursue his or her legitimate interests. If self-interest can be seen as negative, surely freedom to do what you want is an important positive condition for people – freedom from servitude, freedom from control?

For this reason it is hard to think about individuality without addressing the topic of liberty. John Stuart Mill's essay on Liberty has been one of the most important influences on Western society since the Enlightenment. As in so many cases in this book, I can't improve on the original words. As Mills explains in defining what he sees as being the core of liberty:

> *"The object of this essay is to assert one very simple principle, as entitled to govern absolutely the dealings of society with the individual in the way of compulsion and control, whether the means used be physical force in the form of legal penalties or the moral coercion of public opinion. That principle is that the sole end for which mankind are warranted, individually or collectively, in interfering with the liberty of action of any of their number is self-protection. That the only purpose for which power can be rightfully exercised over any member of a civilized community, against his will, is to prevent harm to others. His own good, either physical or moral, is not a sufficient warrant. He cannot rightfully be compelled to do or forbear because it will be better for him to do so, because it will make him happier, because, in the opinions of others, to do so would be wise or even right. These are good reasons for remonstrating with him, or reasoning with him, or persuading him, or entreating him, but not for compelling him or visiting him with any evil in case he do otherwise. To justify that, the conduct from which it is desired to deter him must be calculated to produce evil to someone else. The only part of the conduct of anyone for which he is amenable to society is that which concerns others. In the part which merely concerns himself, his independence is, of right, absolute. Over himself, over his own body and mind, the individual is sovereign"*
>
> (Mill, 1859, Chapter 1)

When we read this view, 150 years after it was published, it still remains a powerful, challenging, and controversial statement: it is a fresh today in its application as it was when it first appeared. Could you find a more compelling touchstone to arguments about abortion, intellectual property rights, or the freedom to express your views on the Internet?

Of course, as is always the case, the devil is in the detail, and the key section in this statement, and the one over which so many battles have been fought is *"the conduct from which it is desired to deter him must be calculated to produce evil to someone else. The only part of the conduct of anyone for which he is amenable to society is that which concerns others"*. How would we define "evil to someone else", or identify something that is "a matter of legitimate concern to others"? Let me restate that: how do you define "evil to someone else" or "a matter of legitimate concern to others"? Of course, it is hard to answer a question like that in the abstract: all the interesting versions of this question come when we seek to apply it to real circumstances. Do you think publishing a racist tract on the Internet is likely to produce "evil to someone else"? Do you consider choosing not to wear a motorcycle helmet is "a matter of legitimate concern to others"? Are both these liberties that should not be allowed? This gets very difficult, of course, as in an interconnected world so many things we do have an impact on others.

In one sense, Mill is offering another version of the argument that Glaucon was making to Socrates. Basically, people should be free to follow their own self-interest, and the only grounds on which we can constrain this are if their activities impact on the rights of others to pursue their self-interest: this might be one way of explaining what we mean by 'evil to others'. Glaucon is saying that we will pursue our liberty as far as we can, and only laws and controls will limit this – in Mill's terms, laws providing the means to ensure we are not harming others.

Of course, Mill is not arguing that it is better to be a crook than to be good. He would have found Glaucon's argument as uncomfortable as we do. But he is arguing that if you want to live dangerously (not wear a motorcycle helmet, engage in extreme sports) or if you want to spend your afternoons at the casino gambling, then, as long as it does not affect others then you should be allowed to do so, even if others do not agree with this way of living. Today we have many grounds on which we can argue that the actions proposed in these examples do affect others – such as having to have medical services ready to rescue and treat you at society's expense; or having your family live in penury because of your gambling debts. It really is the case that the underlying problem with Mill's statement is in its application – the devil really is in the detail – as we are very good at finding reasons why someone else's action impact on us. Is this because we are fundamentally concerned with our own self-interest?

If Mill has had a major impact on Western society, there are many cultures and countries, especially in the Asian region, where the concept of liberty is subordinated to the importance of the community, of society. For an advocate of the importance of conforming to society and the community, we could go to one of the great Chinese Philosophers, thinkers who were developing their views at the same time as the Greeks. Some two and a half thousand years ago, Confucius put forward the view that obedience to the family and to society should be the cornerstone of a good life. In that strange collection of aphorisms and stories, The Analects, Confucius observed:

> *"A young man's duty is to be filial to his parents at home and respectful to his elders abroad, to be circumspect and truthful, and, while overflowing with love for all men, to associate himself with humanity (jen). If, when all that is done, he has any energy to spare, then let him study the polite arts"*
>
> *[jen: Sometimes translated as "goodness," "benevolence," or "love," it is the supreme excellence in man or perfect virtue]*
>
> *"Behave when away from home as though you were in the presence of an important guest. Deal with the common people as though you were officiating at an important sacrifice. Do not do to others what you would not want others to do to you. Then there will be no dissatisfaction either in the state or at home."*
>
> (Confucius, Analects 32 and 43)

However, while Confucius places emphasis on social harmony and the community, he seems to share his underlying view of human nature with that of Plato: he too appears to support the view that it is in our human nature to pursue our own self-interest rather than to be altruistic and think of others, and this is the basis of his comments about appropriate behaviour. He placed great emphasis on the obligations of the 'gentleman' to provide an example for the masses, whose behaviour otherwise would be selfish and uninterested in supporting the community as a whole. Interestingly, it turns one that of his students, Mencius, seemed to have a different view: he believed that people were fundamentally good, but that it was through others – through the socialising process in society – that led them to behave in a less altruistic way.

Both Confucius and Mencius share a similar opinion about human nature in practice, however, even if they have very different ideas as to how this 'nature' appears. This takes us right back to Plato and Socrates, because, as we noted earlier, it was Glaucon, not Socrates, in this dialogue who was presenting this view of human nature. Does Plato, through Socrates, help us? After all, we were hearing what Glaucon had to say, and the more you read philosophy, the more you come to realise that philosophers love to set us up, tell us a story to persuade us we understand the way the world is, and then come up with a telling argument against what we have just read, and hence change our minds. This is, after all, the basis of the so-called 'straw-man' approach: mount an argument that is actually flimsy, and then demolish it to show how smart you are. So, what was Socrates' response?

Well, Socrates was unusually circumspect, and instead of answering Glaucon's question – 'are people only good because they have to be?' – he decides to use the discussion as an excuse to follow quite a different path. Indeed, he asks Glaucon and his colleague as to whether in pursuing the question as to what is the meaning of justice, it might be a good idea to look at what makes a good society (a just society).

He does this very cleverly, and suggests to Glaucon and his friend Adeimantus whether or not it might be a good idea to take a different approach, since:

> *"the inquiry would be of a serious nature, and would require very good eyes. Seeing then, I said, that we are no great wits, I think that we had better adopt a method which I may illustrate thus; suppose that a shortsighted person had been asked by some one to read small letters from a distance; and it occurred to some one else that they might be found in another place which was larger and in which the letters were larger if they were the same and he could read the larger letters first, and then proceed to the lesser this would have been thought a rare piece of good fortune.*
> *Very true, said Adeimantus; but how does the illustration apply to our inquiry?*
> *I will tell you, I replied; justice, which is the subject of our inquiry, is, as you know, sometimes spoken of as the virtue of an individual, and sometimes as the virtue of a State.*
> *True, he replied.*
> *And is not a State larger than an individual?*
> *It is.*
> *Then in the larger the quantity of justice is likely to be larger and more easily discernible. I propose therefore that we inquire into the nature of justice and injustice, first as they appear in the State, and secondly in the individual, proceeding from the greater to the lesser and comparing them.*
> *That, he said, is an excellent proposal.*
> *And if we imagine the State in process of creation, we shall see the justice and injustice of the State in process of creation also."*
>
> (Plato, The Republic, Book 2)

What a masterly line of argument: it is a proposal that allows Socrates to sidestep Glaucon's question, and instead to tell a story about the creation of the state (in a famous passage often called 'the city of pigs'). By doing this, Socrates also manages to return to a much more comfortable role, in which he is asking the questions!

I will not spoil your enjoyment of reading this part of The Republic, but I will tell you a little about where the book as a whole is heading. In this dialogue, which is Plato's major work, Socrates concludes that in a just state there will need to be a number of categories of people – of whom three are critical. Many will be workers, just getting on with their daily business as herdsmen, agriculturalists, builders, shoemakers, and the like. A smaller number will be soldiers, guardians of the city-state. However, an even smaller number will be the leaders of the city-state, and they will be the philosophers, able to discern the truth and to provide guidance as a result of this knowledge. The philosophers will have to lead and guide a state full of people who are – what a surprise! – largely motivated by self-interest, something that the philosophers are able to overcome!

What are we to make of this? Are some people, but only a few, able to transcend their natural impulses and be concerned only for the welfare of others? There is another way of talking about how people act, and a reference to what is often called 'integrity', to being true to yourself (a topic sensitively explored by Stephen Carter, 1997). If you hold strong values, then to act with integrity is not to pursue narrow self-interest, but to act in the light of the values that are most important for you. What are you to make of this? Do you believe that people act according to their values? Or, do you believe that most people are motivated by self-interest, and, if so, does this apply to you as well? If you do, then what can be done to address the need to lead a good life? Do we all have to become philosophers? Perhaps so, if being a philosopher means thinking about the nature of man, what we know, and how we know it. It doesn't have to be a technical exercise, however, but it might mean we have to apply reason to the things that we do, and we see in the behaviour of others. We can engage in some practical reasoning – applying reason to the day-to-day issues of living with other people.

We have covered a lot of ground in exploring the views of Plato, Mill and Confucius. However, each has given a perspective on the puzzle that we set out at the beginning of this chapter: are people individuals at heart, or are they really members of groups, similar in what they seek?

In grappling with the challenges involved in trying to lead a better life (perhaps a 'better life' is one step away from trying to lead a 'good life'), I found a model developed by James O'Toole very helpful. In reflecting on his work as a moderator at The Aspen Institute, he came up with what he later called the 'executives' compass', a diagram representing what he described as 'the four poles of a good society'. In looking at the themes explored in Aspen programs, he saw that some of the issues that participants confront are often in direct opposition to others, a situation we will keep finding throughout this book. Critically, he saw an opposition between individuality and community, the very tension we have been exploring in the last few pages. The other opposition was between equality and efficiency, and this is a topic we will explore in more detail in Chapter 3. For now, here is O'Toole's executive compass:

Figure 4: The Executive Compass

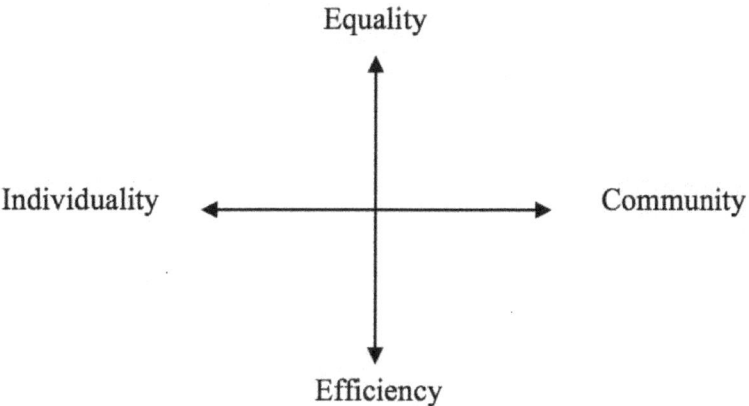

(O'Toole, 1996, p 106)

Each pole is in opposition to the other: each links with those closer by in complex ways. Thus individuality and community are opposed. At one end is 'absolute' individuality, perhaps represented by the hermit (or possibly the socially isolated computer nerd) who interacts with no one else, and whose sole concerns are his or her own. At the other extreme is the person who is a member of a community and without any opinions or ideas – or even actions – independent of those sanctioned by the community (some modern 'religious' communities are accused of requiring their member to behave like this). Of course, most of the interesting territory is in between these two extremes, where we begin to give up some individuality for the sake of increasing acceptance into a community: then the question arises as to what you are prepared to give up, and what remains central to your individuality.

Incidentally, part of the virtue of seeing these two continuums in the form of a compass is that it alerts you to other links between the four extremes of individuality, community, equality and efficiency. Individuality links with equality, and at the same time links with efficiency. In the last chapter of this book, we will try to set out links between a number of extreme positions, and their relative support for one another.

Field Guide Criterion 1:
Affiliation – Individuality versus Community

How can we use the preceding discussion to help you thinking about the life you are leading? At the beginning of this book, I suggested a field guide tells us what to look for – and in this case by identifying the criteria that can help us examine our lives, what we do today, and what we might want to do in the future. In this chapter, we have been exploring a puzzle – the extent to which we are individuals at heart, as opposed to the extent to which we are part of a group. This is a puzzle about affiliation, the extent to which we identify ourselves we relating to others.

To provide a framework that you can use, perhaps we can begin by restating the two extremes of affiliation identified in this chapter. Those two extremes were individuality - where there is no affiliation with others; and community - where the individual is subsumed into the group and loses individual identity.

We came to identify these two extremes through an examination of how we look at ourselves and others, and in particular the extent to which we see ourselves as the same or as different from one another. Since we live in a complex set of relationships, part of the challenge here is to assess what are the criteria that influence us most: the uniqueness of each person, and their right to be treated as such; or the characteristics of the groups to which we belong, and the extent to which our behaviour – and our responses – should be subject to the needs and characteristics of each of those groups.

Given this, the first criterion in our field guide is concerned with helping you find the appropriate balance between individuality and community. In thinking about where you are located on the affiliation criterion, there are some questions you might like to consider:

- Do you see yourself as an individual, following your own course?
- Are there costs you bear because of your membership of a group – and how do you deal with those costs?

- Is the right to be an individual more or less important to you than the need to be accepted by and be part of the group or community to which you could belong?
- How do you deal with the complexity of groups with which you can be associated?
- Is each person a composite of parts, drawn from different communities and groups, or a unique amalgam, no one like another?
- How do you draw the dividing line between individuality and community?
- Is there some point along this continuum that helps you strike the right balance between individuality and community – and what defines that point?

Perhaps there is another way of expressing these questions, which is to ask: Are you happy with yourself - as an individual, and as a member of the various groups to which you belong? If you are not, how would you like to change? What are you going to do to bring yourself closer to that point of balance where you would feel comfortable?

These are difficult questions. Socrates said that the best way to explore questions is to do it in conversation with others. Why not start a conversation about all this? The next chapter will continue our exploration of thinking about ourselves and others, but now moving on to the theme of 'consideration'.

2

Ourselves and Others:

One of the obvious areas in which to question our lives is in how we manage our relationships with others, and particularly how 'considerate' we are. How do we deal with people at work, or our friends, or our family? Should we treat different people in different ways? What do we mean by loyalty? Or being fair? Where does justice sit in all of this?

These were important questions for Socrates. However, when he was exploring justice and fairness, he was living in a relatively simple world: compared to Greece some 2,500 years ago, our relationships with other people are shaped by a far more complex environment than Socrates could ever have imagined. We just have to look around for a few minutes to see that we are surrounded by a dazzling display of the fruits of human ingenuity. The list of the conveniences of modern life is never ending, and we can only be impressed by what people have been able to achieve since the time when Ancient Greece was one the centres of the world.

As we look closely at these technologies and comforts, we should be able to feel reassured. Compared to earlier centuries, surely all this has created a good life? Well perhaps the word 'good' may not be the most appropriate to use here: a good life might be about more than just a comfortable environment. Rather, can we at least agree it has created a better life than that lived in Socrates time, or even a hundred years ago? For those of us living in the developed world, we have better nutrition, sanitation, health and comforts in our lives than could have been imagined when our great grandparents were alive. The quality of life is improving - more slowly - in the developing world. People in almost every country are getting a better education today – again, admittedly some much better than others. In most parts of the world, the physical environment is much better than it was at the turn of the last century, and it is quite realistic to expect this to improve even more in the future. We live in a world where today's physical comfort is matched by the opportunity to achieve even more in the future.

We are also aware that there is a dark side to many new technologies and developments. Nuclear energy can be harnessed to allow us to produce vast amounts of electricity with relative ease, but can also be the source of terrible pollution and also of incredibly destructive weaponry. The mobile telephone allows us to be able to contact anyone, anywhere and at anytime, but it also means that we can be at the beck and call of anyone at anytime. Each technological step forward means that we have to be vigilant about the risks and dangers those steps can entail. Some of these dangers are easily identified; others are more subtle.

Perhaps we can see this clearly when we look at one less familiar example, by confronting what I think is one of the most extraordinary inventions of the human race – an invention that was (and is) quite amazing, and yet one we take for granted every day of our lives. The invention I am talking about is the 'modern formal organisation', a mechanism that has allowed the harnessing of the efforts of tens, hundreds, thousands, even tens of thousands of human beings in a coordinated and focussed way.

Why is the modern organisation so important? Well, one answer is obvious: it is through the power of the organisation that all those technologies and comforts have been made available to us. Without doubt, organisations have contributed to our leading a better life.

However, another answer would be that they are important because they have re-written the ways in which we relate to other people. In that sense, organisations have had an enormous impact on how far we are able to lead a meaningful life – a life that provides us with more than just creature comforts. Why do I say that? Well, to understand something of this second impact of organisations on our lives it might be useful to begin by undertaking an imaginative exercise – rather as Plato did with his dialogue when Glaucon told the story of Gyges ring. As I am sure you have realised, this is a technique that philosophers love to use!

In undertaking this imaginative exercise, what I would like you to do first is to go back in time, and imagine living before the industrial revolution, and even before the formation of large nation states. What would that be like? Well, we would probably be living in a village, part of the estate of a feudal lord. Our relationships would only with people we know and see every day of our lives. They start with our family – and probably we would describe the relationships there as hierarchical and patriarchal. Just as today, we do not choose our family; we simply have to accept it as it is.

At the same time, we are part of a larger group, our neighbours, and these would be people with whom we also have little choice but to 'get along'. Perhaps we work with them in the fields. Perhaps we have a particular role in the village, as the local blacksmith, the house builder, the flourmill operator, or the seamstress making clothes. We live in the same village 'cheek by jowl', and we depend on each other, even sharing the same areas of common land. Again, we do not choose these neighbours, they simply are there. Our world is structured – by the feudal lord who owns much of the rest of the land and who sets our work agenda, by the village priest who marks the rituals of the week and year through the liturgical calendar, and by the cycle of the seasons that determines much of our activity together with the cyclical patterns of life itself.

You can conjure up any variant of the world in which people might have lived before industry, technology and the growth of the nation state began the processes of change towards the world we know today. Whatever the variant, the underlying picture will almost certainly be the same: in any of those pre-modern worlds our relationships were far more limited and personal when compared with today: I am going to describe such relationships as 'particularistic', specific to each person. Would we regard that as a 'good' society? Perhaps not, as Socrates argued that justice was one of the defining characteristics of a good society. In our imagined village world, there would have been law courts and tribunals, but they were largely invisible or out of reach for the majority of the population. Indeed, looking at our imagined picture of village life in the past, it would appear that the idea of relying on the law would have been largely irrelevant at that time. For most people in their day-to-day lives, justice would have been relegated to a hope for salvation in a life hereafter, and what was fair was determined more by the weather and its affects on crops than any legal system. Of course, this did change over time, and if our imagined village was situated in Europe in medieval times, then this was when concerns about rights and equity were beginning to be more widely discussed: however, justice for all, as we understand it today, would have been in short supply.

Let us compare this rather simplistic picture of traditional village life (which in reality was a lot more grubby, challenging and complex than our imagined picture suggests) with the world of the modern organisation, the ideal bureaucratic enterprise. In seeing it this way, the modern formal organisation is characterised by uniform processes, and within that framework we can see that relationships are managed on the basis of universalistic rules and procedures. We expect that when we apply for a job, we will be considered against other applicants on the basis of the same clearly appropriate factors: there will be no nepotism, giving family members an advantage over other applicants. At those times when salary increases are being discussed, our performance will be compared with others against the same sensible and transparent criteria: no special rewards for loyalty to the boss. Working spaces will be allocated on the same basis across the organisation: no special rules for someone who went to same school as the manager. It is a world that is impersonal but fair and just, underpinned by procedures and processes to ensure that everyone is being treated equally and reasonably.

In this, where the formal organization is the exemplar of the way of life in the modern world, the ways in which we deal with other people are mediated by rules and standards that are applied equally to all, (and quite unlike our family life where our relationships are personal and specific to each individual, just as we have imagined was the case for most relationships in an earlier period of history). Managers can come and go, we can change roles, but the fair and equitable environment remains the same. In the same way, the clients of an organisation – customers buying a product or people waiting to be served – they also expect to treated in a fair and just way, probably impersonal but certainly unbiased. That is the modern formal organisation and the world it has created – or is it?

This was the world that William Hyde Whyte described in The Organisation Man, a book written in 1956. As he saw the development of business and the organisation after the Second World War, he believed that people might become like clones, and individuality would disappear (the same kind of world that George Orwell's graphic novel 1984 portrayed). People at work would resemble automata, dressing the same, behaving the same, and undertaking their tasks in a routine and predictable manner. Such a world rubs up uncomfortably against the other, that of family life, which is particularistic and personal. When we contrast these two it is almost as if we would move between two very different realities: that of the family and immediate friends, which still retains some of the characteristics of our imagined world of the feudal village, and that of the impersonal corporation or government department.

If Whyte's predictions of corporate life proved to be rather exaggerated, the contrast his book drew between the experience of working in an organisation and of being part of family life remains. It is exactly the contrast that a legal writer, George Fletcher explored nearly forty years later in his book Loyalty: an essay on the morality of relationships (1993). Fletcher was interested in how we manage our relationships as we move between those two worlds, contrasting impartiality with loyalty, which he describes as the two ways in which we manage our relationships.

Fletcher begins by arguing that we expect that when we deal with people outside our family, decisions will be made fairly, on the basis of universal and impartial principles, as we depicted in our account of the ideal modern organisation. Fletcher suggests that when we are dealing with people with whom we have limited contact, staff in government organisations, the legal system, and the other institutions of society, that "we unquestionably expect certain decision-makers to put aside their loyalties and act on the basis of universal and impartial principles" (Fletcher, 1993, page 162). This is the image of blind justice – applying the law without seeing or taking account of anything personal. However, he warns us that *some* commentators have argued that the same impartial principles should apply to all areas of our lives, even at the level of the family: after all, if Glaucon in the previous chapter was right and it is intrinsic to our human nature to act in our own self-interest, then we should have an impartial system to counter our selfish behaviour towards others.

Fletcher then goes on to explore a very different perspective, that we could manage our relationships with others as we treat members of our family, where loyalty – not a body of impersonal rules – is the critical glue that binds us together. This is based on the views of an 18th Century philosopher, David Hume, who argued that "if every man had a tender regard for another...the jealousy of interests which justice supposes could no longer have a place." What did Hume mean? He is suggesting that if we really cared about each other, the requirement to have laws would not exist – again, as Fletcher argues, taking a view to the extreme.

Two views, and Fletcher concludes that there has to be a balance between them:

> *"[Impartiality] applies in a range of institutions where we confront each other as opaque citizens, as strangers, not as friends and lovers who exact reciprocal duties of loyalty. In the realm of loyalty, playing the lawyer and insisting on justice may well undermine the bonds of loyal sentiment. Equally true, letting loyalties intrude into the proper realm of justice brings about its own form of distortion.*
> *We are left with the question, then, When should justice and when should loyalty prevail?"*
>
> (Fletcher, 1993, page 163)

Fletcher's final chapter is an exploration of this question as he tries to find the characteristics or the definition of that point at which loyalty is no longer appropriate as a basis for how we deal with others, and where what he calls justice – which I am calling impartiality – should take over. In reading Fletcher's discussion in this last part of his book, it turns out that there is no conclusive way to resolve these opening remarks. He is left where he began: he argues that organisations cannot run on the basis of personal links and loyalties, and families cannot be constructed on the basis of impersonal rules. We are still left without a clear answer to the question, other than his belief that this is something worth continuing to explore. The issue is not resolved - for example, does loyalty extend to friends, and if it does so, is there a difference between close and more distant friends? Once again, where is the transition point?

Just as it turns out that Whyte had exaggerated what would happen in his post-war predictions of an organisational world characterised by uniformity and clone-like staff, so I think that it is easy to see that my quick picture is wrong also, and organisations are not the caricature described above. Rather, real organisations are a complex web of relationships, debts, personal ties, alliances, hierarchies and networks. People are linked through common backgrounds and the schools they attended, through past histories and previous agreements and all the tangled sets of connections, obligations and future expectations that these bring. Organisations are concerned with control and influence, with one person determining what another should do. All those principles and processes concerned with establishing fair treatment, justice and impersonal rules set the background, but it is a background against which the realities of the personal and particular relationships are played out. Just as Marshall McLuhan once said the world is becoming a global village, so the organisation can conveniently be described as a set of squabbling neighbours.

It is for this reason that we have to be so careful in what we teach in business schools if we are to make certain that what managers learn has relevance to their lived experiences. We often treat organisations and their processes as if they really are the same as the formal and rather idealised picture we have constructed of them. We talk about them as if they had the attributes of impersonal bureaucracies with all the characteristics that such a perspective implies. Much of the time we analyse performance appraisal, leadership, motivation and working in groups as if we could interact with others on universal and impersonal grounds alone. We don't, and examples of how loyalties and other relationships influence behaviour are to be found everywhere. Have you ever worked in an organisation where there are regular fire drills, and everyone is expected to evacuate the building? Some don't, because they know it is a practice. Then one day, the alarm goes off unexpectedly, and a senior manager keeps working: the rules are clear – leave; the practice is also clear – do what the boss does. Do you leave or not?

Organisational life is far more complex than a simple picture portrays, and we have to be cautious about academic analyses of life at work that give us only a partial picture of the world the manager confronts. The management techniques offered that ignore this reality can only have limited application. We can describe the ideal way to conduct a disciplinary interview, but the real situation has to take account of circumstances and personalities in a way that no formal process can capture. If Whyte's picture was mistaken, then the film Flying High offered a chilling counterbalance as we watched the empty life of a man flying around the world sacking staff he doesn't know without empathy or understanding of their lives or situations. He was impersonal, and for that very reason what he did seemed wrong.

This turns back on us, as we seek to 'do a good job'. Our work is not about abstract things, but about how we relate to others. Fletcher's question about loyalty and where it applies is really a question about how we want to be known, by ourselves and by others. What kind of person are we? Are we to be seen as fair and impartial, exercising the rules without regard to the particular needs of those around us, or are we loyal, caring for those we love and respect? How far does that care extend?

Given that the reality of organisations is rather different from the conventional image, it seems Fletcher's question can be reviewed in a different light. If the experience of organisational life is such that loyalties are as important as any sense of impartial justice, his question about where we should act impartially and where we should be loyal is far more challenging. It is not an abstract question in jurisprudence, but a question about the reality of everyday life at work. Colleagues and staff expect loyalty and impartiality: they expect us to be fair, *and* to respond to their personal needs and expectations: they don't want to be treated like everyone else, and nor do we!

As we have done earlier, one of the ways to explore questions and issues is to present an example, in this case a story to help us examine the challenges of loyalty:

At work, a manager is about to be promoted to the next level up, and needs to recommend someone to take over his former position. There are two choices. One is a loyal staff member, with whom the manager has worked for many years, and from whom the manager knows there will be continued support and hard work to achieve the outcomes the manager wants. The other choice is a newer member of staff, undoubtedly more able than the loyal subordinate, and someone who will continue to rise in the organisation because of her capability, insight and brilliance – even when it is at the cost of others (possibly including the manager himself). Who will the manager recommend? If you were that manager, whom would you recommend?

This is an example that is close to home for many of us. When discussed with managers on university courses, after some hesitation it seems the predominant choice is for the person you have known for years. It is not just a matter of loyalty, it is argued, but also a matter of feeling confident that this person will do the job well and in the way that you want. The underlying concerns – that the other person might contribute more to the company as a whole, or that they might actually do things that suit their future prospects and not yours, and might even push you aside in the process – are less often cited (even if they are factors that are likely to have been influencing preferences). In asking 'Do you want to be loyal, or do you want to be fair?' it turns out that these are complex matters, asking us to confront 'fair to whom, loyal in whose eyes?'

Actually, the problem extends in both directions. We want our children, our partners and others we care about to think that we are both fair and loyal: fair in the sense of exercising impartial justice; loyal in the sense of committing to people as intimate or close friends. In the same way, we want those we interact with at work, in a voluntary organisation, or in our leisure activities, to think we are fair and loyal. How do we pull this off?

Certainly, many people who would argue that excessive regulation and rules to ensure 'fairness and justice' often have the opposite effect. This has been a common complaint about a lot of legislation. In Australia, for example, the Income Tax Act – as a result of its heavily detailed prescriptions in terms of what it does and does not allow – encourages people to look for loopholes. That this is a consequence of detailed regulations that has been known for a very long time: we can go back to the great Chinese philosopher Lao Tzu, who observed "The better known the laws and edicts, The more thieves and robbers there are" (in Book 2, verse 57, of the Tao Te Ching). Indeed, we do not need to look far for examples: just think about your own experience as a child, or as a parent, where the more the law is laid down, the harder it is to keep to the rules.

This leads us to another dimension of our analysis comparing loyalty versus impartiality in managing our relationship with others. In the realm of the family, many of us have learnt that children flourish in an environment where there are strong and clear boundaries, and this seems to be an approach that sits somewhere between the extremes of impartiality or loyalty. We appear to be able manage our children without extensive reliance on rules or regulations, preferring to take time to explain why a certain action is appropriate or not, as opposed to enforcing restrictions. Generally speaking, as parents we manage to ensure that our children behave well, even if the task required to achieve this is that from time to time there has to be a 'serious discussion' or an expression of 'real disappointment' about something that someone has done.

We have covered a lot of ground since we first introduced the contrast between those two imagined worlds: the pre-industrial village where everyone lives together in a closed world; and the impersonal modern organisation where we go to work. As it turns out, that modern organisation is not as impersonal and unbiased as it is often portrayed, and can be often be just like a village too. As a result, what might appear to be a simple distinction in how we manage our relationship with others is also complicated. Rather than one rule for life at home – where loyalty is the key – and another for work – where impersonal justice is the key – the two overlap. We can be 'particularistic', by treating each relationship as unique and dealing with each person individually. However, if we want to be seen as just or fair, then in both arenas of our lives there seem to be at least two alternatives in managing relationships. One is to rely on having detailed rules to guide what we do; the other is to set the boundaries for what is seen as reasonable behaviour, and then be willing to discuss and explore the limits of reasonability as it applies to specific persons or events

Debate over these alternatives has raged for many years in many areas of our lives. An interesting example is in relation to company directors: should the Companies Act set out all the rules to govern behaviour (and the fines to be applied when these rules are not followed), or should the basic requirement be that directors should be able to show that they acted in a 'fair and reasonable manner'? This is described as the contrast between two approaches to regulation – the so-called 'black letter law' versus 'principles' debate. However, whichever alternative is chosen, the underlying concern is about having established clear principles – either set out in great and specific detail, or cast in broad yet all-encompassing terms – principles that are then applied in a universal and impartial way.

Perhaps the most famous and familiar example of the 'absolute principles' approach is utilitarianism. Utilitarianism was a philosophy developed by Jeremy Bentham in the early 19th Century (see Bentham et al, 1987), who argued that the just or fair course of action is the one that gives the greatest benefit to largest proportion possible of the people involved even though this may be at a cost to a much smaller group. The testing of drugs is a good example of this approach. After laboratory and animal testing, a crucial stage in finding out whether a new drug is going to be effective and safe is to test the drug on a sample of people who have agreed to take part in a clinical trial. They may have an illness, for which this drug could be a cure, or they may be healthy people. In either case, they are willing to try doses of the drug, even though there is a risk they may suffer adverse consequences: after all, this is the purpose of the clinical trial. We do this so that the majority of us can receive the benefits of drugs that were tested and found to be good. That a small number of people suffered in drug testing helps ensure the rest of us do not.

Utilitarianism offers a strong contrast to the approach of positive discrimination, which seems to argue in the opposite direction – that justice is achieved if you benefit a small proportion of people who are disadvantaged, even if this is at a cost to the majority. How would this apply to drug testing? The argument might be that we should test drugs on 'normal people' so that their efficacy and dangers can be assessed, before giving them to the minority that have a particular illness? Perhaps a clearer example comes from thinking about progressive income taxation. Those in favour of positive discrimination would argue for increased levels of taxation for those with higher incomes, in order to benefit poorly paid people through income subsidisation or the targeted provision of services. Bentham might well argue the other way round, and suggest that we should have a low flat tax rate for everyone, which would be to the benefit of the majority of income earners, even though that low flat tax rate would result in reducing the benefits to the poorest minority as the total tax take would be lower.

What would utilitarians and positive discriminationists say about the promotion case we outlined above? Would a utilitarian argue that passing over a loyal staff member for the benefit of the organisation as a whole would be the right approach? Would the positive discrimination adherents argue that an appointment to a position should be made to the person who was more disadvantaged? Would they conclude that, probably, the newer member of staff would be the right choice? Or is there another way of looking at their views? Perhaps utilitarians would argue that it would be good to reward loyalty, since it is the loyal members of the enterprise that make it work effectively? Perhaps both would face the same challenges we face in determining the key selection criteria that should apply to the position? As you can quickly see, the trouble with using one overarching principle to determine what to do is that such an approach does not take account of the complexities of individual situations.

There is an alternative approach to using overarching rules, and this is based on recognising that there may be competing principles as well as other reasons for choice, and that we have to use what is sometimes called 'practical reasoning' to determine what is just or fair in specific circumstances. This 'comparative approach' is not the same as the particularistic approach that loyalty demands, however, but represents a step towards recognising that circumstances are important in determining what is appropriate. In looking at circumstances, we are addressing the particular facts and developments that are relevant to making a decision: by this I mean not just the broad context in which something happened, but the specific events that took place, the relationships and history of relationships of the people involved, and so on.

Much of common law faces this challenge: a number of principles in law have been established over a long period of time, as well as how they should be applied (these are the precedents that underpin common law). Using common law in practice, applying the principles and precedents to actual events often means that there has to be a balance struck between two or more competing decisions and a judgement made about what is 'fair and reasonable' in the circumstances. Even in those legislations where there is a bill of rights or a constitution, the principles they contain does not seem to help us deal with the challenge of dealing with circumstances, as they invariably contain a number of provisions: application still requires balancing out the various factors at stake.

The phrase 'fair and reasonable in the circumstances' is a critical one. Fair is often a synonym for 'just', and Socrates seemed to think that creating a just society was one way of creating a good life – and part of his concern with an 'examined life' was to consider what a just society might comprise. As we have just seen, what is just may be determined by one overarching principle, or by a number of criteria. However, reasonable is word that is derived from 'reason', and the power of reason is important – if we want to make sense of things, and if we want to persuade others, reason seems to be a critical skill. Indeed, at this early stage, I want to suggest that one way to explore the path to a good life is to use reason, and reasoning is the underlying bedrock of philosophy. Certainly, using reason is central to the approach of this book.

Applying reasoning to how we relate to others is not an appeal to be scientific. It is not about using the disciplines of physics, psychology or anthropology – even though these may illuminate some important issues. Reason is simply using logic, and since logic itself requires some starting assumptions – axioms – it is also about being clear what those initial beliefs might be. In using the words 'fair' and 'just' we have taken it for granted that there is some basis for accepting that these are important starting points, and can be expressed as the axioms of a good society.

This relates to just one more twist in this discussion that we that turns out to be important when we start to use words like fair or just. What is fair or just often seems to underpin the ways in which we behave without our focusing on explicit or agreed principles. Quite simply, without reading any philosophy or even debating ethical issues, human beings seem to have some innate sense that tells them in broad terms what is right and what is wrong.

It is not clear as to where this sense of right and wrong is to be found – is it really innate, or is it something we learn early on at home and at school? However, it is a factor that plays a part in how we behave: an example comes from trying to help managers think about the quality of a decision they have made. There is a simple test, which can be applied by asking them the question: "would you be happy to appear on a current affairs television show tonight, and explain the decision you have just made". It proves to be a very effective guide: if the answer is 'no', then it is very strong evidence that the manager already knows that the decision is in some sense unfair, unjust, or unethical. Interestingly, it is not always easy for them to explain exactly what is wrong (even if in some cases it is very obvious!). It seems as though we have this internal assessor that helps us make such a judgement, and I am sure that also applies to many things in our day-to-day life.

In the world of organisations, we find that we are expected to exercise both loyalty and impartiality: staff want to be treated fairly, and they want to be rewarded for loyalty. Indeed, these are expectations that make sense for most of us. At times that leads us to act in ways that make us feel uncomfortable, and we sense that in some way we have breached the criterion of what is 'just', a topic that we will explore in more detail in a later chapter..

However, our discussion of the complexities of dealing with people has lead us to identifying our second criterion for this field guide, the consideration continuum, one on which we manage our relationships and which extends between two extremes of impartiality and loyalty. The first extreme, impartiality, is the approach where we treat everyone in the same way – using the same universal rules. The second extreme is loyalty, where we treating each and every person as an intimate friend, and respond to them on that basis. In practice it is impossible to imagine that we could find examples of people who treat everyone impersonally or treat every person as an intimate friend. Rather, as we have described it earlier, real life seems a muddle of the two.

Field Guide Criterion 2:
Consideration – Loyalty versus Impartiality

This second criterion in our field guide is concerned with the balance between loyalty and personal ties, and the impersonal rules and procedures as ways of managing our relationships with others. As the preceding discussion has made clear, we tend to think of intimacy and personal loyalty as being restricted to those close to us by birth, marriage and long term friendships, and everyone else as falling under the domain of impersonal rules.

However, in practice, this ignores the fact that the choices we make are a function of how we see others, and our categorisation of people is not as simple as first suggested. Sometimes, inside the supposedly impersonal worlds of business or the law, we often find the particularity of relationships takes precedence. Perhaps the example given earlier, of how to make a decision about who to promote (or not) is a good illustration of this.

If the two extremes of this continuum are loyalty and impartiality, there are some points in between. We saw that practical reasoning is an approach that can help us work out what to do in particular situations. The basis of practical reasoning is that theory is never enough, as their may be a number of ideals or principles that apply to a particular situation, and we can reason as to what the relative weighting of these should be in each circumstance we confront.

As in the previous chapter, you are invited to think about the relative weighting you give to impartiality and to loyalty. Once again, here are some questions you might like to explore (at least to start thinking, or better, to start a discussion):

- Are you happy that you treat your friends with an appropriate degree of loyalty?
- Are you fair in dealing with the members of your family?

- How do you want to manage your relationships with other people?
- To what degree do you see each person as a unique individual for whom intimacy requires that you act on the basis of loyalty?
- To what degree do you prefer managing relationships using the anonymity of universal rules and policies?
- How do you draw the dividing line between impartiality and loyalty?
- What are some key points for you in this continuum – for friends, for colleagues at work, for team members?
- Does the balance point differ according to the nature of the relationship - close versus distant, or family versus work?

3

Does economics make sense?

In exploring human nature in Chapter 2 we realised there is a simple paradox we face every day – at work and at home: every person is equal, as we are all human beings; yet, in another sense, every person is unequal, as we all have different characteristics and capabilities! This paradox strikes to the heart of a key issue – the allocation of resources: does everyone deserve the same things?

If we start with the first side of this paradox, one of the ways in which we have addressed equality has been to state that everyone – everyone in the world – should have the same fundamental and inalienable rights, rights that cannot be ignored or taken away. The Universal Declaration of Human Rights was issued as a statement by the United Nations in 1948, and contains a number of entitlements that should be available to all. This was on the basis that "All human beings are born free and equal in dignity and rights" (Article 1 of the Declaration). Since that time, the great majority of countries have become signatories to the declaration, even if many of these countries do not ensure all of the rights are available in practice, and others do not grant some rights equally to everyone.

Some of the rights in the Declaration are reasonably uncontroversial. Among the 28 clauses that set out the rights that were identified in 1948, there are nine that stand out – these include the right to life, liberty, freedom from servitude, equal treatment and protection under the law, education, and freedom of thought, conscience and religion. When we speak of fundamental human rights, it would be hard to consider any reason to question any of these nine.

On the other hand, others in the Declaration are somewhat more problematic – are they fundamental human rights, or are they a wish list, a set of aspirations as to what is deemed to be important for people living in contemporary society? Among these are the right for a person to travel anywhere within the borders of their country, to be able to leave their country and to return, to enjoy asylum in other countries, to have a nationality, to own property, to hold a peaceful assembly and to have the right to work with free choice of employment. Why do I say at least some of these are problematic? There are two reasons.

The first reason has to do with clarity over what is meant by some of these rights. For example, to have the right to own property is ill defined. The word 'property' can have many meanings: John Locke explored this when he was writing his treatises on government in the 18th Century, and for him property included things you have picked up off the ground in common areas of land, things you have made, things you have grown. In today's usage, property often refers to land and buildings: does the wording of the Declaration mean to include property in the sense of land or a home? If it does, perhaps this reflects something to do with a level of economic development rather than a statement about what makes us human. There seem to have been many societies in the past where land and many material things were held in common, or were not seen to be owned as such.

The second reason that rights such as these may be problematic is that a right is defined in the Declaration as an 'unalienable entitlement', an entitlement that cannot be taken away. In that sense, rights are neither disposable nor tradeable. However, some rights do not seem to meet these criteria. Article 23 addresses employment, and states:

> *"(1) Everyone has the right to work, to free choice of employment, to just and favourable conditions of work and to protection against unemployment.*
> *(2) Everyone, without any discrimination, has the right to equal pay for equal work.*
> *(3) Everyone who works has the right to just and favourable remuneration ensuring for himself and his family an existence worthy of human dignity, and supplemented, if necessary, by other means of social protection.*

(4) Everyone has the right to form and to join trade unions for the protection of his interests"

In the case of the right to work and free choice of employment, what does this mean in practice? In the modern market economy of most countries, the availability of jobs is determined by competition and cost, not by meeting a fundamental human right. If we look at these economies, much of the time there are simply not enough jobs to go around, and there are recurrent problems resulting from what is sometimes called 'structural unemployment' (unemployment caused by technological change resulting in industries no longer needing certain categories of workers).

Or is it really the case that we cannot find jobs for everyone? Perhaps there are not enough jobs to go around because we take it for granted that jobs should be determined by market forces, instead of requiring that they be provided for everyone.

Certainly we cannot guarantee 'free choice of employment', since there are several positions that have requirements that exclude many potential applicants: few people can work as a doctor, or a lawyer, or an airline pilot. Or does the wording really mean that people should have the right to seek employment, and not be forced into working in a particular way – avoiding forced labour or servitude (servitude is covered separately in the Declaration, in Clause 4).

This particular right raises another problem about the UN Declaration, which has to do with defining who is responsible to ensure rights are guaranteed and protected. The United Nations Declaration is signed by nations – and when a government signs the declaration, it does so on behalf of the nation. However, when we consider how to guarantee a right concerned with the provision of jobs, about a right to work, then this is something that has to be addressed, at least in part, by business. Is business part of the nation? As a corollary of talking about the 'free market', in many ways we tend to treat business as if it is separate from society, rather than an integral part of it. Well, if that statement seems too extreme, then at the very least the place of business within a nation is far from straightforward and deserves close examination.

The free market economy view of business is encapsulated in the statement that 'the business of business is business' (Sternberg, 1994, is a strong proponent of this view). Companies are set up with money lent by shareholders (and debt provided by banks): their task is to provide goods and services in such a way that they are purchased in the marketplace and the costs incurred are less than the income received. The company makes a profit, and can repay loans and give a dividend to its shareholders. Companies are beholden to their shareholders and therefore to 'making a profit', and as such stand apart from society. From this view, companies should not be seen as agencies of government, nor should they be required to ensure the rights of citizens.

This is a view of business that has come under increasing scrutiny in recent years, however. In 1990 Charles Handy wrote a provocative paper that asked the question 'What is a company for?' Companies were established as a legal fiction centuries ago to allow people to raise funds to carry out endeavours that required financial resources that individuals could not provide alone. Now they seem to have become entities in their own right, straddling countries and continents, with their own rules and regulations. Are they a 'world apart?' While the company began life as a convenient fiction, the increasing levels of concern over such issues as environmental responsibility, combined with an emerging view that companies also have to be socially responsible, are forcing Handy's question to be taken very seriously.

What would it mean to see business and companies as *part* of society and not *independent* of it? Certainly we would have to rewrite some of the conventional ways in which we talk about the company as an entity and its operations. Shareholders today are seen as the 'owners' of a company, to whom the whole entity is beholden. Instead, in this alternative approach, they would be seen as no different than banks – lending money on the basis they will get a return. Unlike banks, they would not get any guarantees, and so they would be more like people betting on horse races: looking at the 'form' of each company, and making a guess as to how the 'going' will be in the future. Sometimes they 'win', and get a large dividend, and sometimes they 'lose', and both the value of their bet declines and their dividend is small or non-existent. Perhaps this is the way we should view shareholders anyway: 'owning' a company is a challenging concept, especially when most of the assets today turn out to be the employees.

We would also need to change the way we describe the functions of companies. They would not sell goods and services solely to make a profit; rather, they would sell goods and services in order to meet the needs of customers. At the same time, they would need to make a surplus in order to continue to trade (companies need working capital to cover the costs of goods before they are sold and the income is received), to cover their loans (both banks and shareholders), and to invest in future development. They would have obligations to governments, to society as a whole, to their local community and to the environment. What would be the limits on those obligations? Would they include an obligation to meet the provisions of the UN Declaration, which had been signed by the government? Would this extend to providing employment for all who are seeking work? How would that work?

If we turn to look at some of the other rights in this group I have described as problematic, there are some other reservations that could be made. Certainly, it can be argued some are not always universally and freely available in the sense that characterises the rights in the first group. As an example, the right to live in a country and to hold citizenship has certainly become tradeable. I can 'buy' my visa to live in some countries by showing my willingness to transfer money to that country, and my intention to set up a business. I can also buy my citizenship by selling my skills if I happen to possess a skill "in demand'. As for the right to asylum, this has become extremely complex as political refugees around the world have found when they seek friendly asylum from other countries. Some countries make agreements with each other so that they will not allow asylum to people seeking to go from one to the other. Some countries have policies about refusing refugees because of internal concerns about the ability to absorb them: domestic politics responding to the concerns of voters can ensure the right of asylum is withdrawn. The right to asylum seems to bump up against the right to live in a country and hold citizenship.

While some rights are clearly fundamental and should be available to everyone, it seems clear that there are others that might better be described as aspirations or ideals. However, this is not to suggest that decisions about what constitutes a right should be made on the grounds of ease of implementation, or on the grounds of the costs that including that right would incur. Decisions about human rights are decisions about how we see ourselves and others – and they speak to our view of our common humanity. To have a list of universal rights is one way in which we make real the claim that people are all the same, are equal: the fact that what goes into the list of fundamental rights is contestable is not to disagree with the fact there must be a number of rights of this kind.

Moreover, it may well be the case that not everyone is in a situation where his or her rights are realised in practice. Where autocratic governments or dictatorships run countries that are signatories to the Declaration, they may deny people some of their fundamental rights. Those rights still exist, but are being denied in practice. Indeed, there may be a number of rights we support that are really aspirational, representing the target we need to achieve, not simply what we are able to obtain today.

While there can be difficulties in agreeing what rights everyone should have, and whether they are fundamental or aspirational, there are some other complications that arise. The first concerns the fact that some rights are deliberately made available unequally, as with the rights that are given to some people in order to redress systemic inequalities facing a group. Positive discrimination, or affirmative action, is the obvious example here: by setting quotas or some other mechanism, a disadvantaged group may be advantaged in relation to obtaining work, or getting an advanced education.

Is positive discrimination giving a right to a group in a community, or is it a mechanism to ensure that a right that everyone has is made available in practice, based on the realisation that some groups in the community may be unable to exercise that right through some kind of deeply rooted barrier or hurdle?

In his remarks on loyalty that we discussed in Chapter 2, Fletcher referred to one of the 20th Century's greatest philosophers, John Rawls. Rawls has been one of the most determined advocates of the approach based on justice being achieved through application of impersonal principles. Indeed, he argued that there should be one overarching principle which should be used to determine which path to follow in every situation – in other words, an absolute requirement to ensure justice: his overarching principle is that where inequalities do exist, then they should be of such a form that they give benefit to those most disadvantaged, (Rawls, 1971). An example of such an inequality would be affirmative action – it is an inequality, but one which favours a disadvantaged group.

Rawls is a tough read. He summarises his approach in the form of two principles of justice, the second of which sets out his overarching principle. Those two principles of justice are:

> *"a. Each person has an equal claim to a fully adequate scheme of equal basic rights and liberties, which scheme is compatible with the same scheme for all; and in this scheme the equal political liberties, and only those liberties, are to be guaranteed their fair value.*
> *b. Social and economic inequalities are to satisfy two conditions: first, they are to be attached to positions and offices open to all under conditions of fair equality of opportunity; and second, they are to be to the greatest benefit of the least advantaged members of society."*
> (Rawls, 1999, p 48)

While a real appreciation of his analysis deserves a detailed examination of his book, a simple summary suggests that he is arguing that there are two important rules to be followed if justice is to be achieved. First, that everyone must have the same inalienable rights; and that among those rights liberty is paramount. Second, in an unequal world fairness must be achieved by having measures to ensure equality of opportunity. However, the cornerstone of this approach is to be found in the second part of his two 'principles' – that fairness is achieved by ensuring that social or economic inequalities must meet the requirement that they are of benefit to the least advantaged. His other principles are to be read as more to do with the importance of having rights, providing the framework within which this key principle is to be understood.

It is not my purpose to explore Rawl's approach here, and I am certainly not competent to do so at anything more than a basic level. However, he is worth noting because he helps us understand more about those 'impartial rules' that Fletcher was discussing. Indeed, he is a key exponent of one side of an important discussion about impartial rules. Rawls is an advocate of what Amartya Sen has called the 'transcendental approach' to justice (Sen, 2009). Ideally, in this approach there is one absolute principle that determines what should be done, a principle that must be applied in all circumstances. Is such an overarching principle another form of 'right'?

Certainly, affirmative action is an essential tool in many countries: for example, merely telling a group of Australian aboriginals that they have a right to legal representation, or a right to work, makes little sense if there is no possibility of realising those rights given the conditions in which they live: such rights can only be made practical through enacting some kind of affirmative action program.

It is difficult to assess who should be responsible for ensuring the right to equality of treatment through positive discrimination. Companies may – and do – argue that positive discrimination programs like affirmative action affect their ability to assemble the best possible workforce. When a government asserts in return that this requirement applies to every business in the nation, business people then point out that they compete in an international arena, and that the same requirements are not made in other countries.

A rather more uncomfortable example comes from people living below the poverty line. While there may be government support programs, we still find beggars on the street. Many of us address that concern by giving money to charities, or working for social welfare agencies on a volunteer basis. That still leaves the question, that when we meet a beggar, should we give money to them? What should I do about the handicapped person who is sitting begging at the entrance to a church? I still do not know what to do when I confront this situation, and almost always pass on by. How can I ignore the needs of such a person? Is it my responsibility to ensure that person's rights are being addressed? Is it the government? If the latter, what should I do to ensure that the government meets that requirement?

If that is challenging, I find it even more so when I am travelling overseas, and again I confront a handicapped beggar at the entrance to a church. I do not know the conventions in another country, nor am I in a position to ensure that the rights of the handicapped are being addressed. Is that something I should find out about before I travel?

So far, we have talked about what rights should be supported. Now, consider the question 'Are rights enough?' It may not be enough to have established a number of absolute entitlements. We may recognise the importance of equality, but acknowledging the existence of a right may demand more of us than mere recognition. Indeed, one element of leading an examined life might be for us to subject ourselves to a rigorous review of what we mean by equality, and what we believe we should do in order to sustain equality. Principles are sometimes easier to state than to put into practice.

Tawney, the economic historian who worked on the theme of equality, wrote a book with the same name between 1938 and 1952 (and was still trying to sort out his thinking in 1960!). As Tawney observed, the starting point is to clarify what we mean by 'equality':

> *"On the one hand, it may affirm that men are, on the whole, very similar in their natural endowments of character and intelligence. On the other hand, it may assert that, while they differ profoundly as individuals in capacity and character, they are equally entitled as human beings to consideration and respect, and that the wellbeing of a society is likely to be increased if it so plans its organization that, whether their powers are great or small, all its members may be equally enabled to make the best of such powers as they possess."*

(Tawney, 1952, reprinted in Johari, 1987 p 290)

As he goes on to point out, the first of these two definitions is clearly wrong. Unfortunately, that does not mean because it is right that the other definition is easy to understand or to implement. It is conventional wisdom today to assert that there should be 'equality of opportunity'. The phrase 'conventional wisdom' should alert us to the realisation that we need to examine what this comprises.

What do we mean by equality of opportunity? In one sense that seems easy. Everyone should have an education, and the provision of education should be without discrimination on the basis of language, creed or gender. However, there is some tricky territory to be considered when we want to discuss the provision of 'equality of opportunity'.

An interesting perspective on this comes from Peter Singer. Singer has argued that it is important to go beyond personal preferences, and try to take on a perspective that is wider, a perspective he has called 'the point of view of the universe':

> *"Ethical truths are not written into the fabric of the universe; to that extent the subjectivist is correct. If there were no beings with desires or preferences of any kind, nothing would be of value and ethics would lack all content. On the other hand, once there are beings with desires, there are values that are not only the subjective values of each individual being. The possibility off being led, by reasoning, to the point of view of the universe provides as much 'objectivity' as there can be. When my ability to reason shows me that the suffering of another being is very similar to my own suffering and (in an appropriate case) matters just as much to that other being as my own suffering matters to me, then my reason is showing me something that is undeniably true. I can still choose to ignore it, but then I can no longer deny that my perspective is a narrower and more limited one, than it could be."*
>
> (Singer, 1993, p 231-2)

This approach leads to some interesting conclusions. For example, Singer concludes that equality of opportunity has to be based on equality of capability, by which he means the capacity to think, to have preferences, and even to be able to experience pain and pleasure. If you take Singer's comments literally, equality can only apply if we are talking about others who experience pain and pleasure. This leads to some difficult conclusions. For example, in relation to abortion it appears to be the case that a foetus, at least up to around eighteen weeks, has no capacity to suffer or feel satisfaction: therefore, Singer is able to argue, it is not possible for such a foetus to hold any preferences at all. In a utilitarian calculation, there is nothing to weigh against a mother's preferences to have an abortion; therefore, abortion is morally permissible. Do you feel comfortable with that conclusion? Perhaps this is a case where reason is too strong and that there are other values at stake?

Similar to his argument for abortion, Singer argues that newborns similarly lack the essential characteristics of personhood—"rationality, autonomy, and self-consciousness" — and therefore "killing a newborn baby is never equivalent to killing a person, that is, a being who wants to go on living." This is not an argument for infanticide, but it is an argument about the nature of personhood. Similar arguments could be made about the right to equality of opportunity for severely handicapped people (as Singer argues in his book Rethinking Life and Death: The Collapse of Our Traditional Ethics). Singer is a powerful advocate of the importance of reason in ethics, even when its conclusions push him, and the reader, into confronting some uncomfortable logical possibilities.

At a less emotional level, many people have argued that mass higher education is a misplaced approach to equality of opportunity, as we are in danger of exposing many students to a level of learning (and understanding) for which they lack the capability, whatever their enthusiasm or interest in the subject they are studying. In order to extend higher education to a much broader audience, it is argued that we have had to reduce the complexity of what is taught, and so higher education becomes more like high school, and now it is post-graduate study that has to take on the burden of providing advanced studies. Is that the view of someone like myself, a concerned university teacher, or is that a realistic assessment of the consequences of trying to make higher education available to everyone?

All this makes it clear that in talking about the entitlement to a set of universal rights, we have to be clear about the consequences of 'universality'. In case that seems rather pedantic, a good illustration comes from the enactment of a Bill of Rights and Responsibilities that took place at the beginning of 2009 in the State of Victoria in

Australia. Careful reading of the clauses of that document makes it quite clear that not all of the rights included could be extended to people in prison, for example. Clearly, they should not have the right to travel as they wish. However, should they have the right to vote? Or have freedom of expression? On what grounds do we decide that some rights are suspended for people who have been convicted? How do we decide which rights can be suspended? Clearly, universal and unalienable rights – however defined – may not be applicable to everyone, and the terminology not as inclusive as we might have thought.

Finally, rights can become expensive, and this is where the world of economics obtrudes into a discussion about equality and difference. To say a right is inalienable means it cannot be taken away. However, to exercise that right may require significant expenditure. A little later on we will say more about this, using the example of the costs of the right to vote – elections are expensive. For now, there is a general question: 'How are the costs of ensuring rights going to be met – and by whom?'

One of the 'hot' debates in the second half of the 20th Century was the basis for paying for goods and services, especially which costs which should be met by governments and which should be paid for by users. This debate was given a great deal of impetus by the work of the "Chicago School' of economics, as exemplified by the work of Milton Friedman. Friedman's approach was quite simple – if you want to ensure that things are allocated efficiently, and if you want to ensure that people have what they want, then there is only one mechanism that works effectively, the market. A market based system, Friedman argued, is the only way to ensure that, the economic system is democratic, and fair – as he so aptly put it: "Each man can vote, as it were, for the color of tie he wants and get it; he does not have to see what color the majority want and then, if he is in the minority, submit" (Friedman, 1962, page 12).

Friedman was concerned about efficiency. Like many others who have argued for the central role of the market, Friedman often refers to the work of the Eighteenth Century economist Adam Smith. In a much-quoted passage in *The Wealth of Nations*, Smith observes:

> "*As every individual, therefore, endeavours as much as he can both to employ his capital in the support of domestic industry, and so to direct that industry that its produce may be of the greatest value; every individual necessarily labours to render the annual revenue of the society as great as he can. He generally, indeed, neither intends to promote the public interest, nor knows how much he is promoting it. By preferring the support of domestic to that of foreign industry, he intends only his own security; and by directing that industry in such a manner as its produce may be of the greatest value, he intends only his own gain, and he is in this, as in many other eases, led by an invisible hand to promote an end which was no part of his intention. Nor is it always the worse for the society that it was no part of it. By pursuing his own interest he frequently promotes that of the society more effectually than when he really intends to promote it. I have never known much good done by those who affected to trade for the public good."*
>
> (Smith, Wealth of Nations, Chapter 2)

In using the words 'an invisible hand' in discussing the operations of the market, Smith is arguing that resources will most efficiently be directed through responding to the choices made by individuals in the marketplace. Goods that are made, desired and at a price that is acceptable will be bought; those that are not desired or too expensive will not. This seems to be an argument that resources should be allocated according to needs determined through the open market. While Adam Smith can be read in this way, most readers of contemporary economics are not alerted to the fact that he also had a great deal to say about morality and ethics, as well as about the limits of the rationality of the market system.

The concept of the market – the perfect market – is, indeed, a captivating one. Of course, the advocates of the benefits of the market do stress that it has to be perfect. As Friedman, two hundred years after Adam Smith, notes:

> "*in the complex enterprise and money-exchange economy, cooperation is strictly individual and voluntary provided: (a) that enterprises are private, so that the ultimate contracting parties are individuals and (b) that individuals are effectively free to enter or*

not to enter into any particular exchange, so that every transaction is strictly voluntary"

(Friedman, 1962, page 11)

In some ways, this is an argument about being economically rational. That is to say, we will choose those things that are economically rational for us to choose. If we have needs, and limited resources, we will allocate those resources according to our needs and the cost of the means of meeting those needs. Like many arguments, this one is self-fulfilling. Let's say that I want to buy a bottle of champagne to celebrate something special in my life. There are various bottles available, and some are a lot more expensive than others. Do I choose on a rational basis? Well, what I do is that I decide that I really want to make this celebration special, so I buy a very expensive bottle, even thought this means I will have to forgo some other things in the next week. Is that economically rational? Of course, because I have decided the need to have something special is so high, it is economically rational to spend a lot on this particular item. As I am sure you can see, this quickly becomes nonsense, as we can always find a reason for what we do, and then claim that reason is the basis of an economically rational decision.

That is not the only challenge with this approach. Another is in requirement that the market comprises individuals and transactions are 'voluntary'. Friedman does expand on this, and argues that: "The possibility of coordination through voluntary cooperation rests on the elementary - yet frequently denied - proposition that both parties to an economic transaction benefit from it, provided the transaction is bi-laterally voluntary and informed." Economists seem to have a particular skill in writing things in almost impenetrable language, and that can disguise the fact that reality tends to get in the way of good theory. In most transactions in the real marketplace, neither condition is met. Usually the buyer (and sometimes the seller) is not a voluntary participant in the marketplace – they have a need and they are in the market because they have to meet that need. Equally important, transactions are often undertaken in the face of partial or incomplete information, and this can apply to both parties. When I am looking for work, the transaction is not bi-laterally voluntary: I need work, and while the employer may need someone, it is not necessarily me! When I am in the market wanting to buy a house, I know that I will not be fully informed by the seller (nor do I disclose everything when I sell a house!). Is the free and open market an illusion?

Extremes tend to be useful for theory, and for setting out the territory, but unhelpful as a prescription for actual practice. The free and open market is an important ideal, and it does set out an important way to think about the allocations of resources. Markets are a good way of managing many transactions. In a supermarket today, I am able to look at alternative products, and make a reasonably informed choice as to which I would like to buy given the resources (in this case money) that I have. I may still decide to buy the expensive champagne, but at least I know that I am making a choice against alternatives. Of course, incomes vary, and so participation in the market will be limited by the amount of disposable income a person has: for some, choices may be very limited.

Is there an alternative to the efficiency offered by the market? Most people would say 'No!' The experience of communist regimes, where the state has determined the allocation of resources, has not been a happy one. Lacking incentives to use resources productively, and lacking a fair way to allocate prices, centrally controlled (command) economies seem to illustrate that this is not an effective approach. Perhaps even this is not as cut and dried as it might seem: the Chinese economy is centrally controlled, and they offer a form of 'socialist market economy' that is a long way from Friedman's description. So far, it seems to be working well, doesn't it?

The market has its place, and always has in human affairs. However, to return to our earlier discussion about rights, these should not placed in the market because to do so would make them an item that can be traded, bought and sold, rather than something that is inalienable by either the state or by the individual. There are rights such as the right to vote or the right to have a trial by jury that are accepted as being fundamental and yet these are rights that are exercised at a considerable cost. As we noted earlier, general elections are very expensive affairs. There are some other items we take out of the market that also come at a cost – consider the expenditure that is made every year on the provision of such services as having the law enforced by the police, or to having fires put out by the fire brigade. Are these rights, too, or are they merely government services?

The existence of many services and provisions that are outside the market and where the expenditure is met by government often generates extensive debate about whether or not these areas of activity should be limited, or the right controlled. One argument for fixed terms for governments is that this allows the cost of elections to be kept under control!

A critical area of debate concerns the right to have emergency medical treatment. Much of the data on medical treatment supports the observation that a very high level of expenditure on medical services is incurred in the last three months of a person's life, and that expensive procedures and drugs are used that have only a minimal impact on the extension and the quality of their remaining time alive. It would be economically rational to put a cap on this (and, to some extent, this is implicit in the introduction of private medical treatment coverage). However, this is beginning to put a right into the marketplace, the beginning of a 'slippery slope' that would end not just with the right to emergency medical care disappearing, but all medical care available according to the capacity to pay. The Declaration includes the right to "a standard of living adequate for the health and well-being of himself and of his family, including food, clothing, housing and medical care": however, as medical care provision moves gradually towards the principle of 'user pays', so it is no longer an inalienable right but a service provided in the marketplace.

The very fact that I keep using the word 'right' suggests that this is a class of object that is different from a service or a product. We seem to live in a world where products and services are potentially tradeable in the market, but rights are not. Well, not quite: clearly the fire brigade and the police provide a service – and possibly the law courts as well. We expect that governments will make sure that our rights are protected and ensured, and this will require that some services have to be provided to achieve this.

In all this discussion about rights and the market, does the economic rationalism of a Milton Friedman have a view about what a government should and should not provide? Of course, and as an advocate for the importance of the market, he argues strongly for restricting the role of government, taking the views of Adam Smith on the market place to their logical extreme:

"The existence of a free market does not of course eliminate the need for government. On the contrary, government is essential both as a forum for determining the "rules of the game" and as an umpire to interpret and enforce the rules decided on. What the market does is to reduce greatly the range of issues that must be decided through political means, and thereby to minimize the extent to which government need participate directly in the game. The characteristic feature of action through political channels is that it tends to require or enforce substantial conformity. The great advantage of the market, on the other hand, is that it permits wide diversity. It is, in political terms, a system of proportional representation. Each man can vote, as it were, for the color of tie he wants and get it; he does not have to see what color the majority want and then, if he is in the minority, submit"
(Friedman, 1962, page 12)

At one level, Friedman seems to be supporting Tawney, arguing that the free and open market allows everyone the same opportunity to participate, to sell their labour, and to acquire the goods and services they want.

However, at another level, it is an approach that sustains inequality, since those with greater capabilities will be able to prosper against those with less. If you are skilled and able, you will be able to command a higher wage, and be able to buy many goods and services, whereas if you are less skilled you will have a lower income and your ability to acquire goods and obtain services will be limited. In this sense, the market promotes inequality. The economic rationalist would argue that this is not the fault of the market – if you want to earn more, work harder!

A very interesting commentary on the economics of equality and rights comes from another 20th Century economist, Arthur Okun, who examined what he saw as the necessity for a trade off between economic effectiveness (the free and open market) and efficiency (meeting needs such as rights) (Okun, 1974). He opens his discussion by observing:

> *"American society proclaims the worth of every human being. All citizens are guaranteed equal justice and equal political rights. Everyone has a pledge of speedy response from the fire department and access to national monuments. As American citizens, we are all members of the same club.*
> *Yet at the same time, our institutions say "find a job or go hungry," "succeed or suffer." They prod us to get ahead of our neighbors economically after telling us to stay in line socially. They award prizes that allow the big winners to feed their pets better than the losers can feed their children.*
> *Such is the double standard of a capitalist democracy, professing and pursuing an egalitarian political and social system and simultaneously generating gaping disparities in economic well-being. This mixture of equality and inequality sometimes smacks of inconsistency and even insincerity. Yet I believe that, in many cases, the institutional arrangements represent uneasy compromises rather than fundamental inconsistencies. The contrasts among American families in living standards and in material wealth reflect a system of rewards and penalties that is intended to encourage effort and channel it into socially productive activity. To the extent that the system succeeds, it generates an efficient economy. But that pursuit of efficiency necessarily creates inequalities. And hence society faces a trade-off between equality and efficiency."*
>
> (Okun, 1974, p 1)

Okun argues that rights must be kept out of the marketplace, the viewpoint we were exploring earlier. However, he then goes on to look at some of the other aspects of inequality, and asks how they might be addressed. A particularly potent example is that of income distribution. If the market alone determined income distribution, then the spread of incomes would be wide, and the proportion getting very high incomes would be very small. Why? Simply because the spread of abilities is uneven, and so are the requirements for particular skills and activities. Few people can end up as the Chief Executive Officers of major enterprises; for many people, it will be shop-floor, sales and other less well paid work that will be the only choice available – less well paid because the capabilities are more generally available, and supply exceeds demand.

We may choose to mandate a minimum wage, and even set wage rates for young people, but no country of which I am aware actually requires that everyone be paid the same. In order to bring about some degree of income equalisation, the current and popular approach is progressive income tax – the more you earn, the more you pay in tax (with the tax rate increasing as your income goes up). The income tax thus collected is used to provide benefits and services that are targeted on those earning less: either directly through having income limits on entitlements, or indirectly through government provided services that the more affluent can supplement or bypass by paying for 'private' services.

Part of the trade-off that Okun considers is that between income and tax: we allow tax to increase as we earn more, and accept that this is a reasonable trade-off between equality (ensuring incomes are not too diverse) and efficiency (adding to the costs incurred by having a tax placed on income). However, Okun asks us to take this a bit further. How would we view this system if the actual tax system itself was inefficient? Clearly it will be 'inefficient' in the sense that the money taken in tax is not all distributed directly to the less well off. There are costs incurred in the system through the bureaucratic processes of government tax collection, and the establishment and provision of services. The question Okun asks is "How much inefficiency would you allow before you said the system was not worth pursuing?"

Okun suggests that Milton Friedman is likely to say that he would want no inefficiencies (and would probably prefer a flat tax system anyway). At the other extreme, John Rawls, whose views we have mentioned earlier, might say that he would accept (if he had to) up to 99% inefficiency, since his fundamental principle is to advantage the less well off, whatever the cost. Where would you sit in this vexed debate?

The concept of the trade-off is an important one. In introducing our field guide, we talk about a continuum between two extremes. Every point on that continuum between the two extremes is a compromise, a point at which you are willing to trade-off some of the benefits you would obtain from going to one extreme in order to obtain some benefits of the other extreme. Much of the 'examined life' is about trying to determine what you see as the compromises that are acceptable. In this area of our lives, where economics pokes its nose into our activities, there is a clear trade-off between effectiveness (doing what is required, including, among other things, ensuring rights are provided) and efficiency (minimising the use of resources and the costs of delivering what we are pay for).

Does the idea of compromising make good sense in all areas of endeavour? It seems clear to me that the answer has to be no. For example, in the arts, the concepts of efficiency and effectiveness make little sense (although one accountant who was taken to hear a symphony orchestra was reputed to have commented that it was enjoyable, but time and money could have been saved by having one player of each instrument, and cutting out all the repetition!). To be more serious, it is meaningless to apply the concept of efficiency to artistic works – they simply are what they are. While we might talk about some art being effective in getting people to think or look at things differently, we do not measure art by its effectiveness in achieving specific objectives. Art has its marketplace, but it is valued in its own right, and we cannot use the language of effectiveness and efficiency to help us determine its value.

Does this discussion about trade-offs also mean that we should limit what we see as possible to achieve – that, for example, our desire for equality should be limited by economic factors? Equality, like some of the rights we explored earlier, is an aspirational target. On that topic, we should let Tawney have the last words:

> *"It is true, indeed, that even such equality, though the conditions on which it depends are largely within human control, will continue to elude us. The important thing, however, is not that it should be completely attained, but that it should be sincerely sought. What matters to the health of society is the objective*

> *towards which its face is set, and to suggest that it is immaterial in which direction it moves, because, whatever the direction, the goal must always elude it, is not scientific, but irrational. It is like using the impossibility of absolute cleanliness as a pretext for rolling in a manure heap, or denying the importance of honesty because no one can be wholly honest."*
>
> (Tawney, 1952, p 34)

Field Guide Criterion 3:
Allocation: Equality versus Efficiency

We began this chapter by the challenge we face in allocating resources: do we treat everyone as equal, all entitled to the same, or do we allocate according to ability and effort, recognizing that people are different? In exploring the relationship between how we see each other and the world of economics, the key area of compromise seems to be between efficiency (using resources in the most parsimonious way) and effectiveness (ensuring that we achieve the goals that are important).

In exploring allocation, we introduced the concept of the 'trade-off' between the need to treat everyone as equal, and ensure equality of opportunity, balanced against the need to ensure that we minimise waste and make the best use of the resources we have. The challenge is to determine where to find the appropriate middle ground between the extremes of everything allocated on the basis of efficiency (the logic of the impersonal market), and everything allocated on the basis of equality (the logic of our common humanity).

In thinking about this criterion, here are some questions for consideration and discussion:

- What rights would you ensure are always kept out of the market?
- Is the right to equality more or less important than the need to be efficient?
- Is the market the best place to ensure needs are met?
- What can and should be taken out of the market – and why?
- How do you draw the dividing line between equality and efficiency?
- Are there some areas of endeavour where questions about efficiency and effectiveness are irrelevant – such as the arts: if so, what do you see as the most important of these?

This is one of the hottest areas of debate today, as it is one of the topics that seems to separate political parties and different groups within our society. In exploring these questions, it is always worth adding 'why?' to the end of each question.

This third criterion in our field guide was first mentioned in Chapter 1 when we looked at affiliation. At the end of that chapter we briefly touched on James O'Toole's formulation of two criteria, which he expressed in terms of the 'four poles of the good society': individuality versus community, and efficiency versus equality. The last chapter of this book will return to the question of how these criteria relate, and a more complex model which takes as its starting point O'Toole's four poles.

4

Examining the world around us

I think it was Coleridge, in *The Rime of the Ancient Mariner* who wrote: "Water, water, everywhere, Nor any drop to drink". Today the saying might be "Data, data, everywhere, But not a jot to think". Data is everywhere, or, to use the more familiar word, information is everywhere. That is not the same as saying knowledge is everywhere. Information is not the same as knowledge, because knowledge has an action component to it – it is information that has been assembled, analysed and made sense of, something that we have thought about and as a result gives us the basis for action. I have lots of information about France, its history, geography, cuisine, wines and so on. However, as I have learnt and thought more, my knowledge of how to live in France has steadily grown, and I can plan itineraries that suit my needs, choose foods that I will enjoy, and live well in a previously unfamiliar environment.

Well, I hope my knowledge is growing, but actually how much my knowledge grows proves to be a function of how much attention I devote to thinking about something. This is a challenge, and the reason for this is clear if you think about the weight of all that data surrounding us, as it sometimes seems there is not enough time for that careful analysis that is required. As a result, knowledge is getting less attention.

If knowledge is harder to achieve, then there may be something else that is even scarcer today, and that is wisdom. Wisdom is a term we use to refer to the accumulated understanding that comes out of thinking about knowledge and its uses – wisdom comes from examining what you know and what you think about what you know, the very theme of this book. Wisdom is another level of knowledge, giving us insights and understanding that does not depend on data or specific knowledge. As I have become more knowledgeable about France, so I have become wiser about people from cultures all around the world; I am better equipped to understand places and ways of life different from my own.

In a sense, wisdom transcends knowledge, and allows us to know what to do without having to rely on an already clearly formulated plan or guideline. Perhaps the best known example comes from the story of Solomon being asked to determine which of two women was the mother of a child: both claiming it was hers. Solomon did not know who was the mother – that was knowledge that he did not have. However, he was wise, wise in understanding the ways in which people behave, and realised that if he offered to cut the child in half, one half for each mother, the real mother would rather give up her child but at least have it live.

In exploring information, knowledge and wisdom many people feel they face an up-hill task in working out how to manage the flood of information with which they are presented on a daily basis. While the purpose of this book is to encourage you to ask questions, I am going to step out of that approach just briefly, and in an appendix to this chapter I have said a little about how I manage that overwhelming flood of information. I have placed it there so that you do not have to read it unless you are interested in how I manage my time! Having made my admission, the rest of this introduction to this chapter explores some of the challenges in sorting out information, before moving on to the main topic, which is an exploration of the relationship between technology, information and wisdom.

I have already said that there is a lot of information about, but this is not just an issue of quantity – the rate of growth in amount of information in the world increases exponentially. Many years ago, it was claimed that the amount of information in the world had doubled between 1970 and 1995 – in other words in 25 years we had doubled all the recorded information that had existed before that time! Now, the figures have become close to fantastic: there is claimed to be something like 15 petabytes, or 15 million gigabytes, of new data being added every day, and all that data has meant that we even need new words to describe how much there is (what is a petabyte?). These figures, which come from a survey conducted by Thomson Reuters in 2010, are further set out in their report, where they comment:

> *"The world is awash with data—roughly 800 exabytes. This includes phone calls, security prices, news, company information, social website postings, electronic books and medical health records. And the volume of information is growing. One example of such growth is the Thomson Reuters financial data network, the largest financial real-time data network in the world, which routinely carries 750,000 updates per second of security price changes, quotes and news. Over the past 20 years, our network traffic has increased by 60% every year."*
>
> (Thomson Reuters, 2010)

If you want to be further impressed, an 'exabyte' is a billion gigabytes, a million terabytes!! If you want to know why you should be impressed but do not understand all this terminology, then all I can say is that we are talking about unimaginably large quantities of information!

What do all these big numbers mean for us? At one level, the answer is quite simple – we can't keep up! However, keeping up seems to be a pre-occupation. Many people spend a lot of their time trying to keep in touch, watching the news continuously, reading newspapers and journals, and monitoring blogs and web sites – so busy keeping up that it seems it is impossible to do anything else. All this hard work in keeping up does not necessarily mean that knowledge is increasing, however, as a lot of keeping up is simply updating information. You can do more than just acquire more information, of course: you can also keep up with analysts and consultants, people who will happily do the analytical work for you, providing you with guidance and suggestions as to what you should do. While this has its place I do not believe that this was what Socrates was suggesting when he talked about an 'examined life': he wanted self-examination.

If we really want to keep increasing our knowledge, then we have to make sure time is left for thinking. This means that a critical part of the challenge of keeping up is knowing how to filter and where to focus your attention. One of the ways to do this is to use clever technologies to determine what is significant for us. We can resort to the summaries provided through blogs, networks, wikis and tweets to tell us what is important. These are the technologies that are used to prioritise information for us – and they can be helpful, keeping us 'up to date' on things that matter. However, these same technologies can add yet more to that flood information that is likely to overwhelm us: we have to prioritise the summaries.

As an alternative to those sources that try to summarise what is happening, we can turn to authoritative sources (whether they be stock market analysts we like, or arts reviewers whose opinions we seem to share), and rely on these 'trusted advisers' to alert us as to what matters. However, in ceding responsibility to others to tell us what is important, we are beginning to take a major step away from taking responsibility for our choices. If we want to live an examined life, perhaps we should be more willing to recognise that we are probably our own best-trusted advisers, and if we think about it, know what it is that is important to us.

Another element of ways to help us in the task of keeping up is to find ways of managing our time more effectively. Over the years, there have been a fascinating variety of systems that have been developed to help us in time management. Prioritising tasks is one of the most common approaches: list the things that you have to do, and then sort them out according to a system (A, B and C priorities; or, urgent, very important, and important; or, yet again, drawing on Stephen Covey we should be using the approach of identifying and putting "first things first"). The strange thing is that at the end of the day, so many of the items still seem to be on the list, and progress often appears limited! Why do we appear to be so poor at managing our time? Why is there always too much to do?

Perhaps there is another approach. Instead of just focussing on what needs to be done, we could think about not doing things that do not need to be done! We can actually save a lot of time by not spending time on things that are not important (which was the corollary that Covey was proposing in suggesting we should be putting first things first). While this makes good sense, examination of our everyday routines suggests we often take the opposite approach, and prefer to deal with the easy and routine things first, leaving what is more important to be addressed later – in other words, putting first things last!

Some of the things we could spend less time on are easy to identify – like copious gossip, and extensive discussion at work about what you did outside of work. However, some are less obvious, and for that reason more subtle time eaters! An example of how time can be devoured without even noticing is keeping in touch with the 'news', and it is one that nicely illuminates the information problem.

Being abreast of the news is important for most of us, but this can become excessive as shown by people who listen to the news in the morning, then read their newspapers when they get to work, continue to listen to the news – or read it on websites – and then watch news programs when they get home at night. What is wrong with keeping in touch this way? Well, you might disagree with this diagnosis, but let me reflect on what I think they are doing. As I see it, in large part, they are spending a lot of time listening to five things:

- Breaking news – that is to say information about events that are happening
- Political news – which is news about what one politician is saying about another, or comments on such commentaries
- Media news – news about what is happening in the world of personalities, ranging from pop stars and film stars to football players and media commentators,
- Anticipatory news – people speculating about what might be about to happen (a particular favourite in the worlds of sport, finance and the weather), and

- Business and economic updates – charting the rise and fall of oil prices, company share prices and the statements of chairmen and CEOs

Of these categories, the first is the area that is concerned with new and emerging events, and it is important if you are going to keep in touch with the world around you. However, sadly, there seems to be one compelling characteristic about breaking news, which is that much of the time those initial 'breaking news stories' are often incomplete, and sometimes even misleading, misunderstood, or presented out of proportion. That is inevitable: we don't really know what has happened when something new occurs until some time after the event. So why do we devote time to listening to ill-formed commentary on what has just happened? It might be much better to spend time on the important news stories a little later on, when there is a clearer picture emerging, and as a result actually be better informed. News is an important part of what we talk about with friends and colleagues, and an important element in feeling we are part of the world – understanding and responding to events affecting people around the world: the point is that understanding and discussion may be more worthwhile when done so on the basis of good information, when you are clear about what has really happened and how it has affected others.

The second and third categories are far easier to address. The views of politicians or media people about each other are not really 'news' at all, but are rather conversations, arguments or analyses of the views of people whom are deemed to be important. What makes them important? In part they are seen to be important because the panel discussion we are watching replaces our need to think about what is being said, or what is happening: we hear the commentators exploring the issues, and we simply absorb the information, without discussing it ourselves. They are doing the work of analysis for us, and if we trust these commentators, then that can help.

However, perhaps some of these commentators are important in another sense, as they are people who are said to be important: if we don't question who they are, we no longer have to judge to whom we should pay attention. Importance lies in the imagination of the beholder, however, and can often be somewhat incestuous. A telling example of this inward looking approach is shown by the media's obsession with its own commentators and analysts whose analyses have become tsunami-like in quantity. Today there are whole magazines devoted to giving us information about the lives, loves and clothes of movie stars, pop singers, and other media celebrities. If this sounds a little cynical, it is because all this drowns out the more important news and commentary that are taking place! Equally time wasting is the space that is devoted by commentators to the world of "might happen": as many very clever people have noted before, the one thing you can be sure about the future is that you don't know what is going to happen.

Finally, there is business news. Strangely enough, this can be important. However, the worst place to get information about business is from the news. There are very good monitoring services that can keep you informed on the things you need to know, and even basic technologies like 'Really Simple Syndication' (RSS feeds) can help by automatically advising you when something is said on a topic that is important to you.

The point that is being explored through this example is very simple. If the concern is how to manage information - and time - effectively, then for a couple of days it might be a good idea to stop spending so much time prioritising the work you have to do, and stop trying to keep up with everything that is happening. Instead, it may be more effective to take some time out, and spend the same amount of time looking at what you actually do. What are some of the things that take time but that are actually of no real value or interest? Not paying attention to some things can release a lot of time for things for which real attention is deserved.

I suggest you might consider how you manage the flood of information, and to think about what matters to you (and the appendix to this chapter explains a little about some of the choices I have made). Part of that examination might be to assess the information technologies you use. In fact, one of the recurring concerns we have about the transmission of information and of knowledge has to do with the impact of technology. William Powers does an excellent job in Hamlet's Blackberry (2009) in documenting the response of people to innovations in technology over the centuries, covering such things as the introduction of writing, recording by various devices, the impact of printing, right up to the impact of the digital world. In doing so, he reminds us that concerns about what we see as the impact of new technologies are very old indeed

There are two elements to those concerns. Part has to do with what is seen to be lost. For example, Powers reminds us that in Greek and Roman times, part of the skill of a great poet or orator was the ability to always update and renew the familiar stories – each time Homer told one of his great epics there were often differences from the one before, with elaborations and elements that suited the particular audience and the events happening around them. Then the time came when it was possible to write down an epic – or a poem or a story – then that became the version of the story, and the text became ossified – dead, in a sense – and some of the vibrancy (as well as the immediacy) of its telling was lost. Each new technology seems to leave a gap in its wake: today, we are just as exercised about the loss in personal interaction that is claimed to result from people being locked on to their digital screens. We are constantly being told that young people are becoming recluses, unable to interact socially, caught up in a (decidedly dangerous) cyber world.

In fact, it seems that the degree of loss is never as great as the worriers suggest. Plays and poems have continued to be performed since the invention of writing, and even though we can get recordings of great performances, we often find the live version more engrossing than the recording. Poets still read their poems; and parents still read to their children – and often vary stories or invent their own. Not as much as in the past? Possibly not, but then we have a much richer total corpus of creative work to enjoy, and the new media (print, television, digital) allow other forms of entertainment and exploration. It may not be so much that there are some things that are lost, but that there is just greater variety of alternatives available.

The other concern is a more complex one. New technologies bring a range of consequences, and some are not visible at the time, nor even for many years after. In another chapter we explore the question as to who could have foreseen when the horseless carriage was being developed that its successor, the motor car, would change cities, shopping, and work – almost every facet of how we live. When commentators consider new technologies and their consequences, their focus is often short-term and immediate – it is, after all, very hard to assess what future changes might take place. However, this also suggests that we should be alert to the fact that the purposes for which new technologies are developed may not be the ends to which they eventually become focussed.

Technology is neither good nor bad: technology itself is neutral – it is how it is conceived, developed and applied by people that creates a better or a worse world. However, even that proves to be quite tricky. DDT was a chemical spray that was developed to reduce crop infestation. It proved to be very effective in achieving this aim, but turned out to have some consequences, invisible at the time, which would have prevented its development and deployment if they had been known. DDT did reduce infestations, but at the same time left residual chemical poisons that have lingered for decades, some still to be removed. We may do things for very good reasons, unaware of the implications of our actions, only to regret them with the benefit of hindsight.

We are neither the masters of technology – for technologies do have unintended consequences – nor its servants, as we can make choices. Technology is a form of knowledge – taking information and ideas (often based on theories about the behaviour of the physical world) and seeing ways to apply those ideas to do things, often things that we were not able to do before, or to do them better or more effectively. Technology is about techniques, or 'how to', and is clearly about action. If technology is about practical knowledge, however, there is another form of knowledge, theoretical knowledge. Theory is focussed on understanding, something which may not have practical applications today, but which may provide the basis for applications in the future.

In relation to both technology and theory we are motivated by curiosity, but we can make choices about where that curiosity is focussed. Presciently, back in 1973, Ernst Schumacher in Small is Beautiful: Economics as if People Mattered foresaw the need to re-examine technological development. Schumacher was concerned that many choices about technology and science were driven by greed and envy, by people wanting to develop products and services that gave them greater opportunities in the marketplace, by better satisfying the needs – and especially the wants – of people. He shared that view of human nature we explored earlier, that we are largely driven by our own self-interest, and was concerned that in pursuing our selfish needs we were using up the world's resources, and at the same time creating the basis for conflict and exploitation.

Instead of this approach, he suggested that there should be a conscious choice to go in a different direction:

"The economics of permanence implies a profound reorientation of science and technology, which have to open their doors to wisdom and, in fact, have to incorporate wisdom into their very structure. Scientific or technological "solutions" which poison the environment or degrade the social structure and man himself are of no benefit, no matter how brilliantly conceived or how great their superficial attraction. Ever bigger machines, entailing ever bigger concentrations of economic power and exerting ever greater violence against the environment, do not represent progress: they are a denial of wisdom. Wisdom demands a new orientation of science and technology towards the organic, the gentle, the nonviolent, the elegant and beautiful. Peace, as has often been said, is indivisible–how then could peace be built on a foundation of reckless science and violent technology? We must look for a revolution in technology to give us inventions and machines that reverse the destructive trends now threatening us all.

What is that we really require from the scientists and technologists? I should answer: We need methods and equipment which are

–cheap enough so that they are accessible to virtually everyone;
–suitable for small scale application; and
–compatible with man's need for creativity.

> *Out of these three characteristics is born nonviolence and a relationship of man to nature which guarantees permanence. If only one of these three is neglected, things are bound to go wrong."*
>
> (Schumacher, 1973, p 34-5)

Forty years later, we are still trying to address that shift towards permanence, a term that we have replaced with 'sustainability'. There has been great progress. After decades of illness and pollution caused by inefficient stoves in rural India, there are now stoves being distributed that burn with almost no pollution, heat more effectively, and most importantly significantly reduce the risks of many illnesses. Indeed, India has been a hotbed of such efforts, from developing cheap and effective prostheses through to extending the reach of basic health care through cost-effective and clever systems and delivery methods.

We can make choices about the directions in which we choose to emphasise technological development and enquiry. However, while Schumacher's perspective still makes good sense, it has been complicated by recent approaches to innovation. At the time he wrote, most innovations came from inventions, from researchers and companies seeking to produce a product or service that could be sold in the market. Today we would call that the 'push' approach: develop something, and then go out and market it so as to persuade a customer or client group that this is a better way to meet their needs, convincing them that this is what they should buy. The alternative is the 'pull' approach, where innovation results from trying to find a new way to achieve an desired outcome or meet an existing need, no longer selling to customer but responding to the customer's request.

To be successful in a 'push' world that concerned Schumacher, you need a stockpiling approach – initially in terms of having the products that are required, but, more recently, in having the knowledge that is required (especially protected knowledge in terms of IP covered by patents) in order to meet the needs for which your product or service is relevant. The most successful 'push' companies have proprietary knowledge, and a strong network of partners who work with them. They have been successful because their store of proprietary knowledge was not available to their competitors – they had techniques, blueprints, and operating procedures that were valuable because they gave a company competitive edge over its rivals. All that was hidden away, often protected through patents and copyright.

It might be thought that the 'push' approach is flawed in that the task of the company is to persuade customers they need what the company has produced. In some cases, I am sure this is true. However, some innovators look for products or services to sell to customers because they will provide them with something they really do need, and have not been able to acquire in the past. Prahalad has documented the exciting ways in which Indian entrepreneurs have come up with cheaper versions of such products as artificial limbs or soap, giving access to mobility and health to rural inhabitants (Prahalad, 2004).

However, the 'pull' approach has become increasingly popular with many companies, (see Hagel, 2010). Why is this? Rather than developing something new, and then going out to sell it, 'pull' approaches begin with forecasting needs, and then designing the most efficient platforms to ensure that the right people and resources are available at the right time and the right place. They are based on common 'platforms' which enable a mix of experts to come together from locations around the world to address needs, often by coming up with an innovative approach to a specific problem. These pull models are reactive rather than pro-active: they thrive on change, as they are responsive to needs, not trying to anticipate them.

Companies that still operate in the push world face another difficulty. The kind of knowledge on which this approach relies is codified, explicit and proprietary knowledge, the kind you find in books, guides and manuals. If having such proprietary knowledge has been the basis of the push approach, so today information technology is changing all that. The digitisation of knowledge and its availability on the Internet has meant that it has become almost impossible to protect written knowledge in our digital world, and almost anything is available if you use a search engine like Google – and at no cost!

The pull approach relies to a much greater extent on another kind of knowledge, becoming far more important today, called tacit knowledge, knowledge in your head, learnt by experience. A business does not have to rely on its proprietary knowledge to be successful in a pull world, as the most valuable attribute is being able to draw out and deploy resources from anywhere at anytime – as you need them. This is a world where the customer or client has needs met by connecting with the right suppliers at the time they require them – a world of virtual links and virtual companies. As others have argued, this is the world of the impresario, building up an organisation for just one task, and then letting it fall away once that task has been completed.

As an example, Cisco Systems is an example of a very successful company selling devices essential to make use of the Internet, a typical 'push' business. However, it has begun to explore changes to its business, and in focussing on meeting the needs of customers it has developed an approach where it can evaluate customers' needs and connect customers with more than 40,000 of its specialised partners. This allows Cisco to offer advice tailored to individuals, managing the complete flow of activities from initial consultation through to development, training and implementation, all on a 'one customer at a time' basis. Similarly, InnoCentive began life as an Internet based open-innovation platform that offered challenges to would-be innovators, problems for them to solve. It has moved from a 'push' approach, too, just as CISCO has, by offering a network of connections between innovators and specialists, allowing them to respond to more complex challenges and work with others. They have found that this 'pull' approach supports and encourages teamwork and builds longer term relationships that increase both the quality of the innovative ideas that are put forward, but also enhances the ease with which they can be implemented (see Hagel, 2010, if you are interested in a fuller discussion of these and other examples).

Why does this matter? In a push world, you can make choices that more effectively determine what will be developed; in a pull world, you are serving the needs that come to you, and in that situation, sustainability may take second place to the affluent, the wealthy and the strident who want their needs met now without regard to the issues of permanence that Schumacher addressed. The shift from 'push' to 'pull' may be both more efficient and more effective in meeting the unique needs of each customer or client. However, just as technology is neither good nor bad in itself, so the same can be said of innovation. Again, the challenge is in thinking about what we are doing, and assessing whether or not our approaches are really beneficial.

Not all the issues to do with technology and business are about efficiency and profit. Prestige is another. Many projects are developed at a company or a national level because of the kudos that will flow from their successful completion, as well as recognising that prestigious projects can attract the best minds. Perhaps the most extreme recent example is the CERN Large Hadron Collider that is operating in Europe, a $5bn accelerator that hurtles atomic particles close to the speed of light and then smashes them into each other to investigate the nature of sub-atomic particles – a truly expensive piece of technology. This is certainly a project that is far away from Schumacher's prescription.

It is also the source of yet another dilemma: if we are to assess a project like this, is it reasonable to ask what might be the benefits that will flow from its successfully addressing the physics questions and theories it has been designed to address. There has been extensive discussion of the light this machine might throw on the nature of matter, but leaves open as to what will turn out to be the other implications or technologies that will flow from this work. History tells us this is another impossible task of prediction.

When President J F Kennedy sought to get a 'man on the moon' within a decade, the costs and the outcome seemed difficult to justify, other than to restore national pride following Russia's successful launching of the first satellite round the earth, and the fear that they would also get to the moon first. However, the research and development that was required to achieve that goal had a vast number of spin-offs, and these include:

- The most accurate topographical map of the Earth. This data is used to develop safer navigation techniques and better communication systems.
- Ultraviolet protection suits for people with rare intolerance to UV light, known xeroderma pigmentosum.

- Heart pump based on technology of space shuttle's fuel pumps. It's two inches long, one inch in diameter, and weighs less than four ounces.
- Efficient autos and planes benefiting from NASA wind tunnel and aerodynamic expertise.
- New metal alloys based on research for the space station program.
- Thermal protection blankets used in everything from fire fighters suits to survival gear for cold environments.
- Robots and robotic software with wide-ranging uses that include auto-assembly plants, hazardous material handling, monitoring in dangerous environments, distribution and packaging facilities, etc.
- Lightweight composite materials that benefit cars, airplanes, camping gear, etc.
- Perfect protein crystals grown in zero gravity; used for more pure pharmaceutical drugs, foods and an assortment of other crystalline-based products including insulin for diabetes patients.
- Better understanding of the Earth and its environmental response to natural and human-induced variations such as air quality, climate, land use, food production as well as monitoring quality of our oceans and fresh water.
- Commercial space communication systems for personal phones, computers, video transmissions, global positioning satellite systems, etc.
- Improvements in energy use efficiency.
- More responsible use of air and water in private and commercial buildings.
- Automated maintenance functions for buildings and new lower-cost building construction techniques.
- Smoke detectors for homes and commercial buildings.
- Air purification systems used to by hospitals to provide pure oxygen for patients.

There are a lot more, including some that are more closely allied to developing better missiles and missile defence systems!

To answer the question as to the benefits of the Large Hadron Collider would be impossible today, and maybe there will just as impressive a list. Today that might seem rather unlikely, since this machine is an extension of similar cyclotrons, and is addressing a very specific set of scientific outcomes, but who can be sure? Such projects turn out to be multi-faceted, as the work needed to make the device work effectively often require the improvement of many supporting technologies, which then lead on to quite unrelated benefits, as the Kennedy moon project demonstrated.

However, while trying to assess possible benefits is a legitimate concern, this is to miss Schumacher's point, which is not about the unintended consequences of research and development but about the choices we make as to the problems worth addressing. $5bn addressed to such technologies as the example given earlier – better stoves for cooking in India – could make a massive difference. What is more important – sub-atomic physics, or rural health in India? Researchers will tell you that basic research yields enormous benefits in the long term: in the short term, many Indian children grow up malnourished, with impaired mental functions, their mothers suffering from various illnesses derived from poor cooking systems.

Perhaps a key point in this is 'who makes the choices?' Marx and Engels, in The Communist Manifesto had no doubt that it was those that owned the means of production:

> *"The bourgeoisie during its rule of scarce one hundred years has created more massive and more colossal productive forces than have all preceding generations together. Subjection of nature's forces to man, machinery, application of chemistry to industry and agriculture, steam navigation, railways, electric telegraphs, clearing of whole continents for cultivation, canalization of rivers, whole populations conjured out of the ground–what earlier century had even a presentiment that such productive forces slumbered in the lap of social labour?"*
>
> (Marx and Engels, 1848)

Technology has been extraordinarily successful in the past two hundred years – even more impressive than Marx and Engels saw in 1848. Pragmatism has driven many – but certainly not all – of those outcomes, by focussing on what needs to be done.

Pragmatism sits at one end of a continuum, and pure theory at the other. Pragmatism is where we use technologies to achieve a desired outcome – it might be to ensure better health, or a better manufacturing system, etc. – without having to spend time on the theories that underpin these technologies. Pure theory is directed towards understanding, divorced from any practical application. A pragmatic approach measures value in terms of how far it makes things better, using technologies to increase efficiency and effectiveness. A purely theoretical approach measures value in terms of the scope and depth of understanding, and theories are focussed on simplicity and comprehensiveness. Pragmatism relies on evidence, showing that things work. In contrast, pure theory often requires us to take some things 'on faith', since it often proceeds on the basis of accepting some fundamental principles or axioms, a topic we explored in a previous chapter as we discussed issues to do with science and religion.

Where does wisdom fit in all of this? Wisdom is not concerned with pragmatics, the ability to do things, nor with theory, providing frameworks to explain how things are. Rather it is concerned with a deeper level of insight that transcends specific areas of theoretical knowledge. Wisdom enables us to deal with the world around us without having to rely on what is known and written down, but rather is built up from our experience, our tacit (learnt) knowledge, and can even draw us into thinking about what is better, what is good, and what is sustainable in the broadest sense of that term. Wisdom sits above the continuums discussed in this book. Wisdom is knowledge about knowledge, or to be more precise knowledge about knowledges. It is about the ability to step back from theory and pragmatics and to ask deeper questions about meaning and purpose. It invites us to move away from an exclusive engagement with techniques or knowledge, and to consider why we do the things we do, and what ends we are striving to achieve.

In a world dedicated to progress, it seems that many people see wisdom as having a superfluous or incidental benefit: it is the ability to do things, to be successful that matters. However, a great deal of research on 'successful' people shows that, at the end of the day, their success has counted for little (John O'Neill, 1993). The mantra of progress and more in business seems to be a path that can never be satisfied. The prestigious heads of major enterprises neither seem satisfied with what they have achieved, nor with the salaries they have earned: the drive is always to do more and achieve more. Not surprisingly, the questions that are asked by these same people at the end of a career of business building and receiving ever-increasing income are always of the kind "but what was it all for?"

Many technologies are not only potentially destructive in terms of the uses to which they can be put, but they are also destructive in another sense – in order to test theories and to come up with ideas, we take a pragmatic approach to the world around us. We take things apart, test them, and try to understand how they work in a scientific sense. This approach to the world around us is at a cost to the opportunity to gain wisdom, at a cost to other perspectives on our world.

This is not just about the long debate between scientists and religious adherents about points of view, it is also about what we choose to ignore, or by our actions those things to which we become blind.

This discussion is not able to convey the dilemmas of pragmatism with the same clarity that Kevin Gilbert did in a powerful and confronting poem to be found in his collection The blackside (1989):

Aboriginal Query
What is it you want
Whiteman?
What do you need from me?
You have taken my life
My culture
My dreams
You have leached the substance
Of love from my being
You have leached the substance
Of race from my loins

> Why do you persist?
> Is it because you are a child
> Whose callous inquisitiveness probes
> As a finger questing
> To wreck a cocoon
> To find the chrysalis inside
> To find
> To explore
> To break open
> To learn anew
> That nothing new is learned
> And like a child
> With all a child's brutality
> Throw the broken chrysalis to the ground
> Then run unthinking
> To pull asunder the next
> What do you seek?
> Why do you destroy me
> Whiteman?
> Why do you destroy that
> Which you cannot hope to understand...

Whose knowledge and what kind of knowledge are important? Even if we are to heed Schumacher's call for science on the small scale that is oriented to permanence, accessible and easy to adopt, it is still science in our terms. Are we listening to the world around us, and are we paying heed to other perspectives? The triumph of the enlightenment and the rise of modern science may have come at a cost. In part, some of that cost may have been that we have not paid enough attention to dealing with pragmatic issues – addressing worldwide diseases, for example – while we have focussed on developing new and better theories. Those theories may well help us address practical issues in due course, but there is a lot of very useful understanding today that could be alleviating major problems.

Perhaps there is another cost, also, which is that a focus on science may have shaped how we see ourselves, and our place in the world. We will return to this topic in a later chapter.

Field Guide Criterion 4:
Intention: Pragmatic versus Theoretical

In a world awash with data, with information, it is a huge task to find out what we need to know. It is possible to spend hours every day searching for information, but the task of discovery is never complete: there is always more. On the other hand, our ability to analyse and make sense of that information is also compromised by the scale of the task: we allow others to tell us what things mean, and as we are disempowered from developing knowledge, our level of understanding is similarly limited. We are masters of the art of application – taking what we have been told, and following the rules that has been set out; perhaps we are less masterful when it comes to generating new knowledge, or even understanding the relationship between different knowledges.

The criterion that sits underneath these issues is that of 'intention' – what it is we want to do when we try to sort through information and listen to advice. Sometimes our intentions are very pragmatic, we need to get something done. Sometimes our intentions are conceptual, we want to understand why things are the way they are. So this criterion in the field guide is defined by a continuum that runs, as usual, between two extremes.

At one end is pragmatism – just getting on and doing things because you have the ability to do it. At the other end is pure theory, having knowledge about the world in terms of values and qualities that are one level removed from practical work, focussed on theoretical speculation. Of course, getting on and doing things relies on knowledge that has a theoretical base, even if that is embedded in the practical procedures. Equally, we usually seek to understand things in order to then go on to apply our understanding.

These two extremes have to be linked. Perhaps there is a mid-point here, which is practical knowledge, understanding that is derived from formulating axioms, and then testing the conclusions you draw against the world of action, hard facts and intractable data, having your ideas tested by reason and verified by application, seeking data to prove – or disprove – what is being claimed.

The questions to be explored here are concerned with the intention - what you want to do:

- Do you see yourself as a practical person - good at application of technical skills?
- How much time do you set aside to reflect on what you are doing, and considering how to use those skills?
- On the other hand, how often do you question your understanding of the way the world works, the ways people behave?
- Do you accept, or challenge?
- How easy is it to find a balancing point between these two extremes - would you prefer to be more practical, or more analytical?
- Should we keep journeying from one end of this continuum to the other?
- What does this mean for an 'examined life'?

Appendix: Managing the flood of information

When I asked myself the question 'How can I manage the flood of information that threatens to overwhelm me?' I concluded that I had to focus carefully, and rely on fewer sources. I had a clear objective: I wanted to be able to think, and not use up my time 'keeping in touch' to the extent I had in the past.

This had three elements. The first had to do with news. I gave up television for nearly 20 years (I now have a television again, but seldom watch it). I stopped listening to the news on the radio, and instead I listened to classical music, which is often a lot more enjoyable (but we'll talk more about that later). I still had newspapers delivered to my office, but skimmed over them to see if there was anything worth reading – and most days found nothing except awareness of headlines kept me 'in touch' with what was going on. Why did I do all this: the answer is simple – as discussed earlier, the 'news' only becomes clear with time, which is one of the reasons I started to read The Economist regularly, as it contains a weekly 'news update' that is a little 'out of date', but including a lot of carefully considered information and analysis: much closer to being accurate. Mind you, given its political sympathies, I find it useful to balance my weekly doses of The Economist with a monthly injection of the New Internationalist, a left wing magazine with a very different slant on what is happening.

Second, I decided to review how I should keep in touch with my own technical field. There are many journals that I could read, but in the end, I settled just for one – the Harvard Business Review. Why did I choose that? There were two reasons. First, it is written in accessible English (the kind of English that you and I speak), not the esoteric English that is used by academics, which seems to offer them a cloak for their own uncertainties, and at the same time give their field the verisimilitude of being densely reasoned and analytical. Second, I discovered that the editors of the Harvard Business review seemed to be extraordinarily skilled at picking up what was 'hot and interesting', identifying those pieces of research that really were adding something useful to our stock of knowledge. Like The Economist, the Harvard Business Review is, for me, a trusted source.

Third, I realised that I had to be open to new ideas and directions, and not just in my own field. A lot of the most interesting things that take place often seem to happen on the margin. Of course, The Economist is good for that reason, as it has sections on many areas of the world, on finance, on business, on science and technology, on culture and the arts, and so on. However, I also read The New Yorker, partly because it is so extra-ordinary a magazine: quite literally, you never know what is going to be covered next. I also keep in touch with some blogs and other Internet sources – perhaps my favourite is still 'Arts and Letters Daily', which serves a similar role to The New Yorker. Oh, and did I mention I read books? The book is an extraordinary device, an intermediary between our inner world and the external. In one sense, a book speaks only to the reader, allowing that person to think about what is being read, to reflect on the images and ideas, and to construct their own imaginative understanding. In another sense, the book is also a link to other people – a kind of major Facebook entry, which can be used as a basis for conversation and sharing ideas and experiences.

Of course, I am not proposing you copy my approach. What I am suggesting is that you might like to think about how you manage the flood of information, and what matters to you.

5
Reaching in to the future

In examining our lives, part of the task has to be to look backwards and assess what we have done in the past, and then to think about what we are going to do in the future. We need time to realise our plans and achieve our expectations. Time provides us with a structure to live by, but as we think about time extending into the future, it reminds us that we cannot know for certain what time will bring. Do we have enough time to do the things we want to do? Did we make good use of the time we spent last year? How much time do we have left – to finish this task? How much time to live?

Time is problematic, because it is essentially unknowable, uncertain. There is no possibility of determining when we will run out of our time in the world. An accident, an illness, a terrorist bombing – any of these things could happen today, next week, in twenty years time. We can look backwards and see how we used the time we had. However, when we reach forward and plan what we want to do next, we never know how much more time we have to use. It seems our expectations have to be limited to the extent we have to live with uncertainty about the future.

Time is always with us, running in the background, providing a setting or a context for what we do, giving us a set of signposts as one hour is followed by the next. As an experiment, try taking off your watch and getting rid of clocks for a couple of weeks when next you are on holiday. It is a very liberating practice. Living life without a timepiece reveals some of the ways we relate to time. When we wear a watch, we have instant access to time, which may give us the comfort of knowing where we are in the day. Things happen on time. We know how much longer we will be at work. We know when the film will start that evening. Without a watch, we live in a less structured world, but one where we make the choices about when we do things. We can go out when we feel like it, eat when we feel hungry. Time becomes elastic, suiting our needs, rather than making us conform. This is contrary to our usual experience: rather than seeing time as elastic, our normal practice is to use time as a fundamental basis for being organised, providing a framework to order our lives and our experiences.

Looking at time reveals a central theme in examining our lives – our expectations about what is happening and what might happen next. On the one hand, thinking about time challenges our expectations as we realise that developing plans for the future will always be problematic, because the future is uncertain and ambiguous. On the other hand, using time as a framework gives us a basis to ensure order and control.

Strangely, although it is so important, we do not usually spend a lot of time reflecting on the nature of time. It turns out that there are a number of ways in which time is described. Some are ways of viewing time as if it were available to us like an endless ocean: we talk about having "all the time in the world', that things are "timeless". Some are about the frustrations of having too much time: we are busy thinking of things to do to "kill time". We even speculate as to how time benefits us: "is time our enemy or a friend?" Among these various ways of talking about time, there are two others that provide models for us, familiar ways to help us organise our thinking about the past and the unknown future; cyclic and progressive time.

As I am typing these words, the trees outside the house are losing their last leaves before the onset of winter, and Thanksgiving has just been celebrated. These events remind me of that very familiar model of time seen as a repetitive cycle, epitomised by the seasons of the year. This is the image of time we associate with living things – the cycle of spring, summer autumn and winter – and the natural cycle that goes from birth, through growth to maturity, and then on to old age and death.

We all know this natural process applies to ourselves as well as the rest of nature, but we tend to think about this cycle in slightly different ways as we grow older. First, when we are very young, the idea that we live for a limited time only is incomprehensible, and quite often frightening. Our parents help soothe away the image of our mortality by distraction, and soon, as we grow older and the world becomes more and more interesting, those fears begin to slip towards the back of our minds. Then, as we begin to move into adolescence our hormones take over. We are young, vital, and the world is there for us to take. Reflections on our mortality take a back seat. In the next stage, as young adults, work and family becomes the focus of our lives. We are busy looking after children, nourishing a partnership, and attending to whatever it is that we do to make a living – working for someone else, working for ourselves. For many of us it is later, when retirement looms and children are leaving home, that we begin to reflect seriously on our own life course. We see friends and colleagues getting older, and some die. Our mortality becomes an ever-present feature of our lives, but now less frightening, more natural.

In many Western societies attention to the natural cycle of our lives has been pushed into the background. For younger people, entertainment takes the place of reflection. Lives are filled with games, the Internet and television. Death becomes impersonalised, ever present in television programs and computer games, but strangely meaningless at the same time. You shoot people in a game, and even get shot yourself – but then you start again: there is a never-ending supply of people to kill, and you are immortal! At the same time, real death remains hidden. People disappear, and funerals take place, but we tend to hide the evidence of mortality, so that even at a funeral more and more frequently we find the dead body is hidden away in a casket. We don't see death.

For many adults the concerns they may have about getting older are translated into a focus on the importance of outward appearances, of 'looking good'. To begin with, this is about cosmetic enhancement and fashion. Later the focus becomes more about fighting the evidence of ageing, through regular spa treatments, cosmetic surgery, coupled with an obsession with fitness routines for the body, and, increasingly, for the mind. We are conscious that we live for a long time and are concerned with the quality of our lives, and want to keep fighting the battle to look young, and to keep ageing, let alone death, at bay.

Finally, as we become elderly, we tend to be described as incapable, frail, and unimportant. The elderly fade out of sight, best left to themselves in their own homes: we are unaware that people are dying, because that takes place in the conveniently hidden special accommodation houses, old peoples' homes and the hospice. It seems that here, as throughout our lives, we are trying to keep death at bay, making it as invisible as possible. Is it better to confront our mortality, and accept it as part of life? Or is it better to keep death in the background, so that we can enjoy life as we live it?

In thinking about time in terms of a natural cycle, the contrast between living in a city and living in the country is very revealing. If you work on farm, or living in an agricultural community, the realities of the natural cycle of life are taken for granted. Birth, growth, death, these are all part of the world around you. In the past few hundred years science has increased our understanding of nature, cycles, and the processes of growth maturity and decay. We now understand that our planet has a life cycle, as does the sun.

If you live in a city, these features of life are increasingly at arms length from your day-to-day experiences: perhaps one reason we seem to ignore the cyclical nature of life is that cities are increasingly 'unnatural'. We tend to compartmentalise our activities, focussing on what is happening to us now, not thinking about the other phases of our experience of life.

There may be another reason that the natural cycle seems distant from much of what we do, and this has to do with the increasing importance of another way of thinking about time – time as progress, an arrow always moving forward and signifying improvement, an image central to living in the 21st Century. We are constantly seeking to make things better, improving, advancing, and all that is left behind is the detritus of former, less sophisticated thoughts and technologies. Strangely enough, time as an arrow has an uncomfortable association in science, with our current understanding of the cosmos as the result of a 'big bang', with the universe starting at a fixed point in the past and now expanding for ever.

What is the consequence of this model of time? The catch cry that emerges from thinking about time as an arrow that is always moving forward is that we must continue to progress, to advance, to improve, to do things better. For many people such progress is about improved technologies that ensure the business of living is easier and more enjoyable. However, if the passage of time is an indicator of progress, 'progress' does not necessarily equate with 'becoming good', because a good life may involve such values as consideration for others, equality, and fairness that progress easily ignores. This is why we keep going back to reading Plato's dialogues because the questions Socrates asks are still relevant today. We may have progressed in terms of the comforts of living, but his concerns about what might make for a good life remain the same.

Clearly, technologies, as we discussed in the previous chapter, are neither 'good' nor 'bad' in themselves: it is only the use that humans make of them that leads to them being described them in that way. However, technologies can certainly make the business of living more efficient, more effective. Technological progress has reached the point today where we are able implement technologies that are individualised (meeting my particular needs, safely) and convenient (everything just where you want it, very easy to use).

In the 'time as progress' model, each person's endeavours are framed within the achievement of progress, not the natural cycle of life. We contribute to society, to the organisation, to the family, and that contribution is measured in terms of material well-being and 'fulfillment'. Such progress is clearly beneficial as we have managed to control many dangerous diseases, improved the quality of life, and as we strive to achieve even more in the future. However, just as progress in medical research has kept diseases under control or even eliminated them, so another strand of research is interested in finding ways for us to live longer – to live forever. Is that also to progress?

Every so often, a social commentator or a religious leader – the Dalai Lama is a good example – will question all this focus on moving forward and will ask 'progress for what?' Then we will reflect for a while on the relevance of what is being said, but after a little indulgent discussion on this topic we are quickly drawn back into the dominant ethos where it is important to improve, not to question progress's desirability. However, the questioning is important. Is the goal of progress 'more'? If so, how much more do we want? When do we say 'enough'?

At the very least, there must be a limit to the number of material things we can have, even if that limit is hard to discern as businesses become cleverer at marketing, increasing what we see as desirable in living a better life. I recently saw an exhibition of funeral caskets from Ghana and England, showing that it is possible to commission your own individualised – and often bizarre – coffin. This is having more than others even when you die! Perhaps it is also a way to help us face death, rather than trying to ignore it – those individualised caskets were part of the celebrations of a person's life, in contrast to the mournful services we sometimes see.

There is a further issue here. If the goal of progress is a better material life through increased prosperity, then the question that has to be addressed is 'Prosperity at what cost?' There has been a significant increase in our understanding of the costs of progress in recent years. In part, these have been driven by environmental concerns. Ever since 1962 when Rachel Carson's book The Silent Spring was published, which drew attention to the pollution of the great lakes between Canada and the USA, we have seen a growing recognition that much progress is gained at a cost, in terms of increasing pollution and too great a reliance on a diminishing stock of non-renewable resources. We also understand that we have been radically changing the diversity and range of life forms on the earth, destroying habitats and niches, and in the process making thousands of species extinct. Until recently, natural selection has provided a slow and steady process of change, but we have changed the pace dramatically. As we see these costs grow, so we are trying to find better ways to use our resources, and to shift towards a rather more renewable and sustainable world, utilising alternative energy sources and reducing environmental costs.

Another consequence of progress has been within the social sphere. We may have moved past the child labour of the industrial revolution, and working conditions are immeasurably better than even 50 years ago. However, to be able to reap the rewards of the improved lifestyle that progress brings, adults now seem to be working longer and longer hours; a burden placed on families. Around the world, hours worked per week are increasing in the so-called advanced economies, even while the percentage of unemployed also increases. As a result, time spent with families is referred to as 'quality time', sustained by the belief that 15 minutes with your children today is as good as five hours with them in the past.

At the same time, leisure is no longer luxuriant time, an opportunity for you to sit and look at a view, or enjoy wandering round a lake. Instead recreation has become 'professionalised', another form of work where there is pressure to have the right equipment, the right gear, to cycle, to run or to take photographs: it is no longer a meandering ramble outside of 'time', but another set of ever-increasing tasks and requirements which continue to exact more from us. Vacations become more demanding, as travellers feel an imperative to 'tick off' the sights they have seen and ensure they have been duly photographed or video-recorded, then neatly filed away on return home – and probably never seen again.

Debates about the consequences of progress are not new, and there have been commentators over the centuries who have worried about the physical and social costs of progress. However, in more recent times another cost has been that we have begun to lose our sense of ourselves as part of the natural order of things around us, forgetting that we, too, are just one part of the natural order, and subject to the same cycles that affect all living things.

The natural world is still there, of course, and so it remains fascinating to travel to rural areas anywhere in the world, and observe the effects of the seasonal cycle on what people do. While holidaying in France I spent some time in farming communities: on one occasion, I loved discovering that there is a French cheese – Saint Marcellin – which has a variety matured in time for harvest, rolled in ash. The cheese is delicious, and I wondered why the cheese was rolled in ash – was it to add some further subtlety to the flavour? Actually, it was done so that when it was being eaten out in the fields during the harvest, it wouldn't attract flies! In a world where most cheese is mass-produced throughout the year, these subtleties and nuances can disappear from view.

So, there are these two familiar views of time. First, there is the view that we live in a world where time is measured in terms of the natural cycle, albeit that this cyclical view of time is seen less clearly by many of us than was the case in the past. Second, ever present today, is the view that we live in a world where time is understood of an ongoing measure against which we measure our achievements in terms of progress. As we look at our lives are we trying to progress, or are we living in accordance with the natural cycles of life?

While the contrast between these two models of time is important, there is another way of looking at time, which is time as it is experienced. In this way of thinking, there are only three points in time. There is now, the present – for me the moment at which I am writing, and for you the moment at which you are reading these words. The 'lived in now' is both our only real experience of time, but also a most fleeting thing. Now keeps slipping by, and what is happening now goes into the past, the second point in time. Experientially, time is only 'now', and yet most of what we know is about 'then'. Of course, that past is useful - looking back into the past can help us identify the things we have done before and think about the changes we want to make in the future. As we think about what we want to do, that future will only come to pass if we take steps now to bring about those changes that examining our life has suggested.

When we adopt this way of looking at time, the past appears like a huge repository, a vast warehouse, full of all sorts of stuff. Some of that material is derived from things we experienced. Other material is passed on to us from others. Technology has changed our view of some of that past material, fixing and freezing what happened then. As a result, we can see and hear ourselves as we were: photographs have existed for a long time, but now we can look at ourselves on film or in a video. This has to be one of the oddest things we can do, to look at ourselves from the future, see our observable selves, and yet be unable to step back inside and be ourselves again. We become a foreign country, a place we have visited, but a place in which we no longer can claim to belong. "Yes, that's me! I wonder what I was thinking then. It's so hard to believe that that was me. Look at me now!"

When we look backwards, everything that is in the past is already gone and irretrievable. We want to give some order – and perhaps some meaning – to what has taken place. To do this, we use dates to sort things out. Some times actual dates may not be so important, and we rely on identifying those things that were 'significant' and highlight them as we review what has taken place. To put things in order may be tidy, but it does no more than that. Is the past interesting to re-examine? Of course it is, it is essential to do so. However we cannot alter the past – only reinterpret it. The only projects worth undertaking if we want to change, if we want to lead a good life, an examined life, have to be forward looking, even though they are based on reflecting on the past.

That leads us to the third element – the future. Just as the past is always out of our grasp, so is the future, because by the time we have a hold on it, it is no longer the future, but the present. Hard to explain, but in some sense we do not experience time, but merely live in it: inhabiting a fleeting sense of now, and everything else a necessary creation of the mind: either a 'memory' that we have constructed, or a future that we can imagine.

What is this strange thing called the future? It is the object of our plans and aspirations, but it only makes sense when it is here and no longer ahead of us. Most of what we do is aimed at having an impact beyond today, and if we are going to assess the value of that impact, we have to carefully consider how the environment in which we are planning to act might have changed by the time our actions have had their effect. Projecting into the future has to be at the core of striving to lead a good life – the use of the word striving implies we are seeking to do something more tomorrow than we have done today, that we have a plan to be different and to do things differently. However, as we think about what we mean by the future and how we might be different then, there are two techniques that can help us – looking at trends, and using future scenarios.

We need techniques to assist us, because it is impossible to predict the future. If that sounds ridiculously obvious, it is because in practice we are surrounded by people who are quite happy to tell us what the future holds in store. The statement that non-one can predict the future seems to be transgressed almost every day. Concerned analysts tell us that if we allow our children continue to play too many computer games they will grow up as socially isolated adults, unable to deal with other people face to face. Investment specialists advise us to put our money into particular projects, or otherwise our superannuation will not be large enough when we retire. Human resource experts tell us that we should not look for employment in accountancy in the future, as this area of work will be taken over by computer systems. How can they know such things? To come up with their advice, they may be relying on trends and developments to assist their thinking, but they cannot know what is going to happen: indeed, forecasting the future has a very poor track record.

Well, perhaps it is important to be careful about what is meant here as there is a great deal of difference between the impossibility of predicting the future, and the very real ability to examine trends and assess likely changes and developments. By using the word 'prediction' we are talking about the ability to tell us something that will happen with certainty: no-one would accuse meteorologists of predicting the weather tomorrow accurately, but we are quite happy that they give us reasonably good estimates – and they do, most of the time!

In other words, if we are not able to predict the future, we are certainly helped enormously by looking at trends and developments. I am fond of using demographic projections to illustrate this element of the future. While no-one can predict how many people will be alive in 2050, or what the age profile of France will look like in 2025, demographic projections, based on current fertility and mortality rates, combined with assessments of probable changes, give us a reasonable basis for saying that it is likely there will be around 9bn people living in 2050, and that France will have something like 30% of its population aged 60 years or more.

Here the operative word is 'likely': much could happen that could change these projections – although to date demographic trends seem to change relatively slowly and, surprisingly, the impact of pandemics of one kind or another usually have only a limited impact on broad projections. There is one – glaring – exception to this in recent history, and that has been the impact of HIV-AIDS on the population figures for Africa in the last 20 years.

In the same way that demographic projects are useful, so many technological trends often seem fairly robust. It is likely that computers will continue to get faster, able to do more, and at the same time become smaller for at least the next few years. More controversially, it is likely that genomics will have a major impact on medical care – both in prevention of illness and in dealing with various chronic and acute conditions.

The task of assessing trends and developments is essential – for our lives, and for the worlds of business, government and not-for-profit organisations. We do need to have some idea as to what is likely to happen. We need those projections so that we can plan, marshal resources, and put in place contingencies. Indeed, with the wealth of data we have today, it would be foolish – almost irresponsible – for any organisation not to spend time trying to read where things seem to be going. Of course, trends and developments are themselves merely another way of using the image of progress. We read trends as a form of progressive development – things have been increasingly like this, and therefore in the future that will be even more the case.

However, we cannot rely on trends and developments alone. We know enough from history to be well aware that uncertainty and unpredictability never go away! Yes, there may be so many million elderly people in the USA in five years time, but …… In our thinking about tomorrow, we have to take account of that word 'but'.

Part of what constitutes our uncertainty about the future is that we do not know today what we will know tomorrow. A particularly interesting perspective on this comes from reflecting on Einstein's perceptive comment that "We can't solve problems by using the same kind of thinking we used when we created them". His comment has two corollaries. First, we do not know today the consequences of what we are doing today, the effect of the approaches we use, the limits of the theories on which our plans are based. Second, we also do not know today what the new theories or approaches will be, so we are unable to guess how we might address the unknowable problems we are creating right now! We will think differently tomorrow – but we don't know how; we are doing things now that will change the world – but again, we don't know how.

If this is sounding very esoteric and confusing, let me give some examples. Gutenberg's development of printing in the 15th Century is often cited as one of the great innovations in history: so, what was important about what he did? Was it printing the Bible? Actually, he began his printing career producing Papal indulgences for monks to sell, a process much faster than handwriting, and one that proved to be financially very successful. He then turned to printing Bibles, and the few hundred that Gutenberg printed cost him more than he made in selling them – he died broke!! However, the importance of what he did was neither printing indulgences nor the Bible, but rather the consequences of printing, which could not have been understood at the time.

What printing did was to fundamentally change the world. First, the aural tradition was dealt a huge blow – even though it took centuries for the full impact to be felt. Instead of listening to stories and histories, words became 'frozen' on the page, and texts lost their flexibility. The second consequence was that printing changed the dynamics of access to ideas: instead of documents being held by the privileged few, mainly religious scholars, printing was the first step towards the universalisation of reading, writing, and education. That change was a key step in the transformation of power, control, and the nature of society. None of all this could have been foreseen by Gutenberg, nor his contemporaries.

Similarly, when some excited engineers put an internal combustion engine into a carriage (thereby creating the horseless carriage), their interest was in making the carriage independent of the horse. However, as the horseless carriage moved beyond being a curiosity and into the omnipresent car of today, so it in turn transformed the way cities grew and were structured, how we worked, how we shopped, and our experience of the world. Those engineers were technologists, trying to improve a vehicle and a means of transport: they might have anticipated better roads, road networks, and motor car technology, but the broader changes in society were the more important consequences that no-one was considering at the turn of the century.

Today we have the all-pervasive Internet that is likely to lead to equally momentous changes – which, once more, we cannot predict. Some of those changes will be problematic, and, as Einstein's comment suggests, we may not be able to identify those changes today, nor be able to solve them using what we know today.

There is a lot more to be said about developments such as these: we first addressed issues to do with science and technology in our lives in Chapter 4, and we will return to this area again in later chapters. For now, I would like to consider another technique that helps us think about the future – and this is an approach that is based on scenario analysis.

Scenario analysis is a way of thinking about the future through developing a set of realistic yet alternative ways in which things might turn out. Scenarios are coherent, consistent pictures of possible futures – each one describing a particular direction that the world might take. They might remind you of those novels that were popular a few years ago which had multiple endings, each ending a result of choices you made as you read along.

Scenarios are not attempts to predict the future, but each scenario is a realistic story about a future that could develop: they are usually focused on some date in the not too distant future – say ten years ahead of where we are today. Scenarios are not predictions, but they help us think systematically about what the future might hold in store. The techniques of scenario analysis are not important to explore here (I have added a brief appendix to this chapter to explain the approach further, and you might find it interesting to read more on the topic – see Shell, 2010, or Peter Schwartz, 1988). Rather, my purpose in talking about scenario analysis is to suggest that by developing a series of realistic scenarios for the future, it is possible to do a number of very useful things in relation to the 'unknowable future'.

One important consequence of scenario thinking is that it does encourage us to think more deeply about what is happening today, and allows us to track what is changing, and begin to discern what might happen as a result of those changes. Each future scenario is the result of something happening between now and the future: in technical terms this is the 'driver' of a scenario. Drivers are deep-seated agents of change, and using scenario analysis encourages us to ask: "what is happening today that might change the world as we know it?" This takes us back to the discussion at the beginning of Chapter 4, where we explored the importance of getting beyond the trivial news and analyses with which we are presented on a daily basis, and digging down to see the underlying trends.

While scenario analysis might seem to be a matter for business people only, it can also help us think about the future from a personal viewpoint. If you want to plan to change your life in the future, using scenario analysis to think about how the future might develop can be very helpful. Actually, we do this quite often, without using the word 'scenario'. For example, you may be thinking about buying a new home. In order to make a good choice, you consider two or three alternative ways this might be done – buying an apartment in the city, buying a small inner city home, buying a larger home further out, or even in the country. For each of these choices, you think about what life might be like. You even take the approach further, and contemplate how your life would be under some quite different broad scenarios – they might include the impact of an economic downturn on your choices, or the consequences of increasing limitations on your mobility through age, etc.

In talking about scenarios in relation to an examined life, I am inviting you to think about might happen carefully and analytically. Scenario analysis is one of the most powerful ways we know to help us think about the future. While it remains true that we can't predict the future, we can think about the future in a systematic way. There is great virtue is asking yourself: 'how do I want to live in the future? It is a hard question, but considering future possible ways in which the world might develop can help.

I have said there are two ways of thinking systematically about the future – either through examining trends or through scenario analysis. Of course, there is at least one other way of understanding or making sense of the future, and this is to use a framework based on belief or faith. We may not know what is going to happen in the future, but we may be willing to take it on trust that there is a source of understanding that will tell us what we need to know.

Taking things on trust, having faith, is a complex thing. Some people seem to think that faith is the exclusive preserve of religions. However, I think it may be useful to think of faith in a different way. When we say we have faith in something (and it can be a person, or a way of understanding the world), it means we accept the truth of what is being said (or the honesty of a person) even though we do not have the objective evidence to support that acceptance, because we trust the source. In that sense, I would like to suggest that science is just as dependent on faith as is religion (see Lightman, 2011 for a very interesting commentary on this). If we accept the teachings of a religion, it is because we believe that the truth has been revealed to us through the teachings or writings of a prophet. If we accept the findings of science, it is because we believe that the tests of empirical research can confirm the theories that are developed, even if there are many unanswered questions about what is meant by facts, observation, and so on.

Indeed, science is more demanding than that. If its practitioners believe it makes sense to describe the world in terms of such things as atoms, sub-atomic particles, strings, multi-universes and dark matter, most of us are in no position to challenge these ideas: we don't have time to check all the empirical research that is being done, and we take it on faith that other scientists do. Actually, these ideas are formulated as theories, ways which have been developed to make sense of our physical environment, and they require our provisional acceptance: for the time being, they are the best way to make sense of the world, and we 'make do' with them until something better comes along. Thomas Kuhn explored the paradigms that underlie science, and the ways in which we accept – we have faith in – the current paradigm, until it is replaced by a better one (1962). We examine the world of very small things, and the universe, with instruments whose readings it is claimed reveal the 'truth' of these ideas and constructs. We develop theories to explain what might be the basis of our world – physically, chemically, and biologically – and then we dream up ways to test those ideas. As a result of this approach, science has been like a cornucopia, making possible so many of those conveniences we referred to at the beginning of this book.

In the same way, for those who are religious, there is a dimension that cannot be described or seen, a dimension in which they may choose to believe in such things as God, souls, and a life hereafter, and even, for some, angels, heaven and hell. Scientists point out we cannot 'test' these beliefs or this other dimension: many find 'proofs' that satisfy them nonetheless. We have a framework that gives meaning to our lives, one that deals with the mystery of our place in the universe in a way quite different from that of science. In fact, in many respects, these two frameworks are not incompatible, just uncomfortable for many people (some scientists are happy to see the two systems are compatible, see, for example, Davies, 1995). People with religious faith can develop theories to explain what we cannot 'see', too, and look for 'tests' of these ideas. Great prophets, like great scientists, help us reinterpret our world: the consequences may not be found in new products or activities, but they may be equally important in allowing us to ascribe meaning to the world around us, and our place in nature.

Both religion and science rely on faith and reason – faith in accepting the fundamental axioms of science or religion, reason in being able to convince yourself and others that there is evidence to support your faith. In emphasising that faith must be complemented by reason, it is helpful to address the 'test' advocated by Karl Popper many years ago. Popper realised that over time theories are often replaced by new theories that explain more, or explain things more effectively. Insofar as this is the case, then we should always regard theories as 'pro tem': they will hold until they are replaced by something better.

Given this, he argued that the only test you can make of the validity of the claims of any theory is to seek to disprove it (Popper, 1959): if faith is the basis of science and religion, then you either accept the ideas ('blind faith'), or you find some way to see if you demonstrate they are not true (if you cannot disprove the ideas, the theory, then, for the present, you have reason to accept it). Such acts of disproof have to take place in the world of apprehendable reality – and that proves to be as challenging as the theories themselves. However, we are ingenious, and can often find a way to demonstrate that some thing is 'demonstrably' not the case. Of course, proponents of science and religion claim that each other do not understand why their forms of faith and disproof are correct and the other is wrong: but surely that is exactly what we mean as being the basis of faith.

Faith helps us deal with the future. It allows us to believe there is a degree of certainty about the future that is not available to us in any other way. Religious faith allows us to comprehend and deal with a world in which we have a finite mortal existence. For some, it gives them the certainty that we continue to have another existence outside of that time on earth. This is in strong contrast to science, which allows us to comprehend our physical world as something that exists and continues independent of us and our desires and concerns, and does not allow that something might happen to us outside of our physical time on earth.

To disprove theories or beliefs we need to exercise the skills of reasoning, a topic we introduced in the previous chapter. Our ability to reason is a precious tool: it allows us to develop knowledge and to acquire wisdom. It is part of the bedrock on which our 'examined life' rests, and the underlying justification for the projects we develop for the future.

To reason is to use logic, to rely on the conventions of the syllogism. In a funny way, we are back to Socrates again, for the most famous example of the syllogism seems to be:

Socrates is a man
Men are mortal
Therefore, Socrates is mortal

How strange to think that these three simple lines of logic are one of the major the building blocks of reasoning, and provide such a powerful tool! Yet it is only through reasoning that we can bring ourselves to testable propositions that allow us to feel comfortable about our faith, our knowledge of the world. Reason provides us with the tools to deal with this complex thing called time.

Why do we have to grapple with all this stuff about time and the future? Well, to lead a good life is both a matter of reflection and of action. We can look back, and think about what we have done and make judgements as to whether or not this has been 'good'. However, to lead a good life is not just to contemplate, nor just to plan, it is to act. To act is to conceive and realise a project for the future. Yet here is another of those paradoxes. Lao Tzu is famous for saying "a journey of a thousand miles begins by taking the first step". The wording is important, as Lao Tzu is often mis-quoted, and people sometimes believe they are quoting his remark when they say 'a journey of a thousand miles begins with the first step'. The key words in Lao Tzu's famous quote are "by taking" the first step. The journey into the future has to commence with action now, even if the project as a whole is conceived as running into the long-term future. To summarise, a good life begins today, but it can only commence if now we reflect on what has happened in the past and conceive and commence a new path to follow in the future.

If you, like me, are finding this topic of dealing with the unknown hard work, we can both take comfort from the fact that so is everyone else who tries to think about time and the future!

One of the first pieces of guidance we developed in this field guide was to recognise the importance of trade-offs, and that a good life cannot be developed through certainties, but through exploring how to find some kind of balance between incompatible extremes. This is the material of practical reasoning – reasoning in the real world – where there are no universal answers, but rather methods to make sense of what is otherwise a world of conflicting priorities.

How has this discussion of time helped us in determining another criterion against which we might want to assess ourselves as we continue to lead an examined life? For much of this chapter we have explored the idea that we have expectations about who we are, and how we fit into this world around us. In looking at models of time we can see there are two rather different perspectives that we can employ: there is a choice to be made between seeing ourselves as just one among many other creatures that exists in the natural world, subject to the same processes and changes as do all other creatures, and experiencing the same life cycle; or, alternatively, as unique in the world, constantly marching forward under the banner of progress. In looking at faith, we can see there is another choice, which is to see us as subject to the impersonal rules of the universe, or as unique in another sense, as living within a world that takes out of the natural order and locates in a realm that is beyond our understanding, only accessible through revelation.

While these are important, there may be another element of how we see ourselves in the world, which is to look at the nature of our expectations. All the frameworks we have just summarised – the two models of time and the religious and the scientific views of the world – all these can be contrasted with a perspective that suggests the world around us is unknowable and unpredictable. In other words, in order to make sense of how we see our place in the world, we might argue there are two extreme approaches. At one extreme are those whose view is one of absolute confidence – they know their place in the world, as scientists or a religious adherents, they understand what is happening around them, and they accept the limits of what can – and cannot – be done. Some at that extreme might even claim our free will is illusory. The other extreme is those people who are willing to live without certainties or clear frameworks, without any firm beliefs about the way the world is and how it will evolve in the future. This is the extreme of having no solid ground on which to stand, inhabiting a world of ambiguity and indeterminacy. The trade off in dealing with who we are and what will happen to us is finding the balance between the extremes of absolute confidence against absolute uncertainty.

Field Guide Criterion 5:
Expectation: Confidence versus Uncertainty

This last chapter has been wide ranging, starting with models of time, moving on to a commentary on the bases of science and religion, and finally looking at uncertainty. The theme within all this is that of 'expectation' - how do we manage to make sense of what we know about things?

At one extreme, there is confidence - we know things are the way they are because we accept and believe in the truth offered by a way of looking at the world. That certainty comes from empirical science for many people today, but for others its comes from religious revelation. It is also supported by how we see the passage of time – as something predictable and definite. It is, at the extreme, unquestioned confidence.

At the other extreme is doubt, always questioning and never satisfied that we can be confident about anything. Some philosophers have pushed this extreme to its limit: nothing can be certain!

As with other criteria, most of us occupy somewhere in the middle ground. We do accept that many things are known, we are willing to take some other things 'on trust', but we are also willing to live with some degree of ambiguity or uncertainty: after all, that is one of the reasons we are willing to read a book like this! The challenge is determine what level of uncertainty we are willing to accept.

Thus the third criterion in the field guide is finding the appropriate balance between confidence, knowing the way things are, and uncertainty, being able to address and feel comfortable with ambiguity.

As in previous chapters, here are some questions for you to consider:

- Do you see yourself as part of the animal kingdom, subject to the same 'laws of nature' as are other living things, or

- Do you see yourself as part of God's world subject to a received body of absolute principles and laws?
- Is there some place between these two that makes sense for you?
- Alternatively, do you see yourself as an agent of change, able to make things different from the way they have been - to progress?
- How do you perceive and make sense of your mortality?
- Is progress an important goal, and in what ways can we evaluate progress?

As a result of thinking about these questions, do you want to learn more about science or religion, and become more comfortable with knowing how things are, or do you want to become more sceptical, living with more uncertainty and ambiguity?

Appendix: Scenario Analysis

Scenarios are pictures of possible but realistic futures, ways of thinking about the future without trying to predict what will actually happen. One important facet of scenario analysis is the recognition that each scenario we consider is the result of something happening, a 'driver', something that pushes the future in a particular direction. Drivers can be simple, or they can be very complex. As an example of a fairly simple driver we could look at the so-called 'war for talent'. What is this about? The term refers to the situation we are experiencing today where there is a shortage of skilled people in various areas of employment who have to be paid well to attract them into an enterprise. At the same time, that same 'war' refers to senior executives continuing to pay themselves - and others with skills in demand - more and more, so that their salaries will rise faster than those in others. This war for talent is likely to lead to a future where there is an ever-increasing income inequality. Thus the war for talent could be the driver of a scenario called 'a grossly unequal world'.

In this scenario, populations would be split between a very small proportion in each country with extremely high salaries, working around the world, and able to pay for what they want, and a very large proportion on relatively low salaries who are stuck working where they are, and dependent on government services and support to meet their needs. In fact, such a scenario was popular a few years ago, and still makes sense today. If this is a scenario we want to consider, we can track that 'war for talent' and see if it is becoming stronger (and hence the scenario is more likely), or diminishing (and hence the scenario is less likely).

Scenarios are not just developed as an intellectual exercise. Scenarios can be used to help make choices about how to act in order to increase the likelihood of a preferred scenario emerging. It is possible to influence the future, and if you have thought systematically about what possible futures could emerge, you are then better placed to assess the effects of interventions - whether they are at an individual, business, industry or government level. The converse of this is also true. Wise analysis of scenarios helps you identify risks and threats, and ways to manage risk and anticipate contingencies more effectively. The oil industry, which has been a leader in this scenario business for many years, has been very smart in assessing how energy sources and resources are changing, and how this may impact on their businesses.

Scenarios can be developed at a personal level, particularly if you are interested in achieving the goal of an examined life. One step towards that goal can be to ask: "what are some scenarios for my future that I could consider?" One might be to live in another country for a few years – where you could pursue a new career, learn a new language, and broaden your understanding of the world around you. Another might be to work for a voluntary organisation for a few years, giving back to the community, and making use of your skills to help others. Another might be to work extremely hard in your present position for five more years, to build up a surplus that would then allow you to make a choice between alternatives the, or allow an extended holiday. You can consider each of these scenarios as alternatives, thinking them through carefully. This would allow you to explore what you could do, and thereby help you think about yourself and your aspirations – and maybe highlighting some of the challenges you will face in following each of these paths. You could go even further, and take each of these scenarios and think about how the broader environment might change and what impact this might have on each choice – scenarios for each scenario!

There is yet another use of scenarios. Scenarios allow us to contemplate future opportunities – and develop plans before they even occur. To illustrate that idea, suppose we have a scenario that suggests that hydrocarbon power for land transportation (petrol and its variants) will be replaced by electrical power (fuel cells): actually, this is moving from being a possible scenario to being a likely scenario! To an entrepreneur, this is a gold mine: what would be needed to ensure effective access to fuel cells and their components? How would they be recharged? Where? What could be done with the spent fuel cells? Equally interesting, what opportunities exist inside the gradual phasing out of petrol engines?

Once again, this example is focussed on the business side of scenarios. Suppose we consider social scenarios. One might be that we look at a current trend – that we are increasingly connected into networks and communities, but these networks contain many people who are not physically close to us – and we can see this trend increasing even further in the future. This would mean that the use of the word 'community' becomes a term to describe like-minded people, and not used to describe those living around us. Using this trend as a driver, we can imagine a future in which most of our links are with people with whom we have no physical contact. This scenarios suggests that there are some interesting possibilities in 're-grounding' people, so that they are also connected to those who live around them, as well as having links into these other like-minded communities. How could this be done? What are the opportunities – and how would people respond to be 're-grounded'? Would they want to take sup such an opportunity?

As explored in the chapter, it seems that developing scenarios is a powerful way to help us think about the future. It is true that we can't predict the future, but we can think about the future in a systematic way. Those who do have found many benefits - but in particular, scenarios present the possibility of seeing opportunities in the future. Entrepreneurial managers can anticipate how to make use of these insights to ensure their businesses prosper in the long term. You can use scenarios to think about how and why your world might change, and what you might want to do in these different possible unfolding futures. Scenarios will not tell you how your children will develop in the future, or what will happen to your superannuation investments, but they will help you think about how your children's world, or your, might change. Why not start using the approach now!

6
Acting strangely

If much of what is being argued in this book is about moderation, about finding a balance, then one of our approaches has to be that we need to understand the extremes in order to know what the area in the middle looks like! A lot of our childhood is spent learning the rules of the game of life – whether they be in sport, leisure, schoolwork, or in our relations with others. We are warned off extremes – those are dangerous territory. However the socialisation process of childhood is an important part of the preparation we need to undergo so that we can be let loose in the world. How do we learn to do more than just be obedient and conservative once we become adults?

As adults we find that conformity is still the foundation of many of the ways we interact with others, and being different is a path that is discouraged. Work, especially in business, is essentially impersonal and rule bound, a topic we first explored in Chapter 2. A useful way to think about organisations is to see them as devices to ensure conformity, with processes to ensure that the rules are followed and innovation is minimised. Even our leisure time pursuits are often conventional: when thinking of travelling somewhere we tend to follow others in choosing our holiday destinations. In our family lives we are often involved in bringing up the next generation by repeating the same patterns of socialisation that we experienced. There are good reasons for this: we benefit from what our parents had learnt, and we believe we can help our children! At the same time, it is interesting when we look at teenagers wanting to break free and express themselves. What we see is that they dress and behave just like other teenagers doing the same thing – the rebellious statements made through grunge jeans, piercing and dreadlocks seem to be just another uniform, badges of conformity showing membership of the group!

If we are going to step outside the first stages of socialisation and push back against conformity, then there has to be some kind of incentive to change. People are a complex mixture of desires and abilities, and while socialisation and conformity keep many of these manageable, even under control, those same desires and abilities are also the forces that can push us into breaking some of the constraints that otherwise stop us being different. This is tricky territory: we do not want to become socially undesirable, or even end up like Socrates, but perhaps we do want to do something new, explore a new way of being. While the pressure is on us to conform, to lead conventional lives, every so often we want to break out, to 'act strangely'.

That word 'strange' is revealing, because from time to time we realise that we can be strangers to ourselves. Away from our usual surroundings, or sometimes just in the privacy of our own mind, we sense there are some attributes of ourselves that we find both fascinating and yet slightly unrealistic. We dream about ourselves living a very different lifestyle, a story we have seen at the cinema, or being that stranger we sometimes glimpse beneath our usual self. It is as if there is an element of ourselves that is waiting to be released, just like the glamorous spy in the film, the clever detective in the murder mystery or even the great inventor saving the world with a stunning idea.

Is all this fantasy? One way we can look at this is to realise that the very forces that contribute to us leading a routine and predictable life can also breed resistance. Our very predictability arouses in us a desire to be different. Here is a curious feature of our unexamined lives: even though we may not see it as such, our desire to break out is a reaction to being at one extreme on a continuum that runs from conventional behaviour through to be a non-conformist. Perhaps we were born with a non-conformist streak within us, which has simply been suppressed through the normal avenues of socialisation.

Are there people who live at the other extreme on this continuum? One source of insight might come from considering those who operate closer to the other end of the spectrum, the artists and inventors of this world.

Artists are often vibrant examples of non-conformists. Among them are those who are wilfully excessive, their lives and their art often making us disconcerted and uncomfortable: 'mad, bad and dangerous' as some have described them. For that reason, they often fascinate us, but it is a fascination tinged with fear of what they are saying and doing. We read about the behaviour of a group of artists like the Pre-Raphaelites, the Bloomsbury group or the artistic community in Paris in the 1920s and 1930s. We are fascinated today by their lifestyles as much as by their artistic expression, and we are less confronted by their 'new' ideas: so many of their radical thoughts and concepts have been completely taken up by the mainstream, and it is difficult to understand the initial power of such radical ideas. Stravinsky's Rite of Spring has become accessible in a way that the tomato throwing audience at the 1929 premiere in Paris would be stunned to discover. When we look at the behaviour of some of these artists in the past, we take comfort in the fact that we would never behave so excessively, except ....

Artists have done more than illustrate very different ways to live, of course. They are an interesting group to think about: through viewing their work, we are invited and encouraged to understand that any of us can choose to lead a life that is more creative, to reveal aspects of ourselves that conformity has banished. We can choose to make lustre ware pottery; to dress up each month as soldiers and re-enact great battles of the past: in fact, we can be ourselves, whatever that means for each one of us. Artists show us that individuality is both important, and can be part of our lived experience, allowing us to use that liberty that John Stuart Mill had claimed as a right for us all "The only freedom which deserves the name is that of pursuing our own good in our own way, so long as we do not attempt to deprive others of theirs or impede their efforts to obtain it" (Mill, 1859, p 14)

Creativity and art is not just about liberty, however, about 'doing your own thing'. If we choose to open ourselves to art and allow a relationship to develop as a result of hearing, seeing, playing, or performing art, this may have surprising consequences. Sometimes the experience of art gives us a new perspective on the world around us, through a picture showing us a new perspective on something we thought was familiar. Sometimes it can expose us to emotional extremes, or help us uncover feelings that lay hidden below the surface, or release an expressive side to our character that had been suppressed before. If these new perspectives are revealed, then it is likely because of our willingness to open our hearts and minds to a new experience. It is as if that vertical line in the Johari Window, explored in Chapter 1, has been moved to the right, and some of the elements of ourselves previously inaccessible to us have now become known – or at least the area of the unknown has been diminished. We are allowed to become more in touch with our emotional responses, to show how we feel, countering the forces of conformity described in The Organisation Man.

Through art and artists, we can benefit from their challenge to conformity, through new areas of behaviour becoming possible. This is a never-ending exercise. Every generation has the opportunity to try a new path, sometimes supported by creative minds, sometimes suppressing activities seen as too edgy: the tight-lipped Victorian era gives way to the 1920's flappers; the 1960's hippies give way to the conservative business era of the 1980's.

The arts fulfill another role, which is to help us document and restore what has been lost, no longer seen or no longer observed because we have learnt a different way of seeing or making sense of things. This power in artistic expression is to be found partly through are enabling us see things from a different perspective. John Carroll suggested a compelling example to make this point, by getting us to look at a Holbein painting of a dead Jesus (Carroll, 1993). Pictures of Jesus are usually symbolic, referential, and idealised: they are there to remind us of God, of the miracle of resurrection, of the importance of faith. Holbein throws all that aside and shows us someone who is dead. It is a cold, hard painting, all the more powerful in the 21st Century when we work so hard to hide death. The stark power of that painting is extra-ordinary, as the artist reminds us to look again, and says 'remember what this is about'.

Creativity does not belong wholly and solely in the domain of artists. It may be realised in developing a hitherto unacknowledged way of delivering a social service, as much as in the development of impressionist painting. The arts are more likely to do more than create something new – on occasions the arts can shock, provoke, or make us rethink what we believe. The consequences of a piece of art may be coincidental, or may be deliberate, as we saw with Holbein. Just as religious symbols can be challenged, so the virtues and symbols of war can be torn away and reassembled by an artist who exposes us to another perspective. For example, stories of war have a long history – consider these lines from Homer, where he tells us about the experience of being in a battle. He is telling you about the reality of war, not an idealised story like The Dambusters or The Guns of Navarone. Rather this is one that focuses on injury, pain, misery, and death:

> *"Then fate fell upon Diores, son of Amarynceus, for he was struck by a jagged stone near the ancle of his right leg. He that hurled it was Peirous, son of Imbrasus, captain of the Thracians, who had come from Aenus; the bones and both the tendons were crushed by the pitiless stone. He fell to the ground on his back, and in his death throes stretched out his hands towards his comrades. But Peirous, who had wounded him, sprang on him and thrust a spear into his belly, so that his bowels came gushing out upon the ground, and darkness veiled his eyes. As he was leaving the body, Thoas of Aetolia struck him in the chest near the nipple, and the point fixed itself in his lungs. Thoas came close up to him, pulled the spear out of his chest, and then drawing his sword, smote him in the middle of the belly so that he died;"*

(Homer, The Iliad, Book IV)

Galleries are full of pictures that symbolise the glory of war, the achievements of the conquerors. Even many war memorials manage to focus on the heroism of combatants while acknowledging their deaths. Homer has ripped all that away, and says to us clearly, unemotionally, that this is not what war is about. It is a horrible, inhuman activity, and in so doing he frightens us, makes us realise that this is not where we want to be: it is an approach that makes you say "No, never again!"

That is not to say that the remembrance of those who died in wars and war memorials are in some sense 'wrong' or inappropriate: far from it. Recently I was in a small town where wreathes were being placed on a memorial to the dead of two world wars. The symbolism was not about glory, but about honouring and remembering those who had served their country: flags were lowered, and heads were bowed. These were people who had died for the sakes of others. Homer was as concerned then as we are today to keep fresh in our minds those who have died for the sake of a country, an ideology, or even a cherished value like democracy or freedom. His concern was not to go beyond that point and paint war itself as glorious: he wanted to remind us it is a nasty, unpleasant business. We have managed to hide so much of that today as we watch smart bombs blow up buildings in far away places from the comfort of our arm chair: anaesthetising war by distancing it is a way to make us forget what Homer was telling us – perhaps we still need a Homer today, to keep that message fresh and clear.

One film that touched many people in my generation was Apocalypse Now. There is an enduring image in that film as Lieutenant Colonel Bill Kilgore is leading his fleet into rural Vietnam, guns blazing while Wagner's Ride of the Valkyries is blasting from his helicopter's speakers at maximum volume. As the helicopter continues on its flight, so you may recall one of Kilgore's more memorable lines– that evocative phrase "I love the smell of Napalm in the morning" – as he watches the fire bombing of a village. Francis Ford Coppola makes you cringe with pain and embarrassment – is this what the liberation of Vietnam was about? Do you still believe in honour and glory?

The impact of some art may be less deliberate and confrontational. Manet's glorious series of pictures of Chartres Cathedral do not shock us, but, if we are drawn to them, encourage us to see and at the same time feel the effects of light and season on something as solid as a building. Once seen, for many people those pictures are not forgotten, simply because they helped us see another reality of something that was always there.

Works of art invite us to do more than just look, they make us see – make us examine hard and long. It is as if they pull off the blinkers we normally wear, that stop us really seeing things in the way we have become accustomed: they re-present the world to us. In many cases the artist is drawing our attention for a purpose: the artist is saying 'can you see what I can see?'

Sometimes the impact of art is immediate, and the image or the words are pushed right in your face: you cannot avoid understanding what is being said. Holbein, Coppola and Homer were all like that, direct and to the point. However, there are many occasions when this re-presentation does not work as immediately or clearly, and many of us still cannot actually see what we are being shown. There is a language – languages – in art, and if we do not understand them, then we can miss what is being conveyed. The image is there, but it is not accessible, and we have to work at understanding what is to be seen.

Representational art is more accessible for many of us, as the principal objective being to give us a copy, a facsimile, of a moment frozen in time, of what was being observed. However, once we start looking, we discover that those that seemed merely representational often speak to more than just a reproduction of an image: a portrait becomes a portrayal of character, an insight into what the artist 'saw' in that person that went beyond the physical image. Some portraits are mere flattery, it appears, and they make a person look good, or beautiful, or even rich. However, we are often drawn to portraits that are far from flattering, that tell us something about that person's character. Many self-portraits are a good example. Perhaps that insight is amusing – the subject comes across as slightly dissolute, or has a wandering eye. Sometimes that insight is more challenging, and the portrayal is of someone cold, hard, vindictive. The subtleties of how we read those character traits are themselves worth exploring. Today we use the term 'emotional intelligence' to describe the ability we have to 'read' a portrait: alas, we all know we can make mistakes about people, and I am sure the same is true about some portraits.

Contemporary art is rather more demanding. In a gallery we may see a huge black canvas; another nearby is entirely white. Is that art, we wonder? Perhaps we go into another room where we see a video playing on a television set: we watch for twenty minutes – it is a camera on a beach, staying in the same place, filming waves breaking on the shoreline. What does it mean? Art like this is to be 'seen', to be experienced, but does that mean it has to be understood in an intellectual sense? Art may be engaging, and the engagement may lead us to respond in ways that were far from the artist's intention.

Music is even harder to talk about. I grew up listening to classical music, and wore out records of Beethoven, Sibelius and Brahms. Those majestic pieces of music spoke to me, but not with a language that I could relay to others. It wasn't just the familiarity of rhythm, but rather the shapes, and the architectures of sound built up and broken down over long passages of time. At the time I had no idea that Beethoven's Eroica (3rd) Symphony was such a radical piece of music – it simply held me enthralled, evoking some deep seated feelings of triumph, glory, achievement and disappointment.

Today I find music still plays an important place in my life: as I listen, I experience emotions, some easy to identify, some less immediately understood and some discordant and abrupt. If I listen to Shostakovich's 8th String Quartet, I feel how it expresses the pain of war, of lives lost, of meaningless deaths and destruction. If I listen to Berg's Violin Concerto, I cannot find the words to describe what it means to me, nor even understand my response, but it draws me in nonetheless.

Music, even more than visual art, offers another challenge to us: aural wallpaper, Muzak, elevator music, present but effectively unheard. Music can be entertainment, and by repetition can become like a comfortable sound pillow, fun, but no longer speaking to us. I can remember the first time I heard Mozart's Eine Kleine Nachtmusik. I loved it! Now I just hear a tune that has been overplayed in hotel elevators and restaurants to the point that I don't listen, and don't really want to hear it. Perhaps it was always just a nice tune. A stronger example is Vivaldi's Four Seasons, similarly played to death in public places around the world: it was such a revelation, recently, when I sat and listened to it being played live, and watching the sheer physicality, the fiendishly virtuosic demands for the violinist's role, heard it again, fresh, new, and realised what a glorious piece of music it really is – and remembered too how well it spoke to me about time and the cycle of nature, that cyclicity in time we considered in Chapter 5.

Why have I dwelt on these personal experiences? In part, this is because I believe that spending time with the arts and opening ourselves to what they offer can help us in the task of thinking carefully about our lives and ourselves. The arts can fulfill many roles for us. They can operate at the level of escapism by taking us away from the here and now; and sometimes, by appealing to our senses and our minds, they can transport us into another realm. At other times some art can stretch and extend our perceptions and thoughts, pushing us into new territory if we are willing to listen to their messages. They can encourage us to act strangely!

Perhaps all this is familiar to you. In that case, I think a rather more interesting question may be whether or not it is possible to release the artistic impulse within ourselves, to allow ourselves to become creative, to simply 'do something different'. Like you, I am sure, I have battled with this within myself for years. I love photography, but my photographic endeavours often end up looking like another exercise in collecting! For years I have been trying to photograph an example of every different bird that lives near me, building up a collection of birds I have seen. That Field Guide to the Birds of Great Britain is still there somewhere in my head! I would like to draw, but I am afraid to put pencil to paper: I feel those giants of drawing whose work I see in museums wherever I travel looming over my shoulder, smiling at my scribbles. I would love to write fiction, but so far I have deleted four attempts at novels. I want to stretch myself beyond the activities of my normal life, and yet my steps towards doing so have been tentative and weak. Maybe a requirement of creativity for many of us is that it takes time. Time away from the normality of a life you have constructed, time to clear your head to make room. In the case of this book, it was written as a result of having the glorious opportunity to have the space to take time out.

Socrates isn't able to stop me in the street, and question me as he did the young men of Athens – and I should probably be grateful: he would quickly expose my hesitant self, and would question me on how I could claim to have lived an examined life if I have never ventured far enough away from home to know how my life could change. Our engagement with the arts and creativity highlights our need to examine how far we are living a life of routine (close to that 'organisation man' that Whyte described) – almost certainly an 'unexamined life' – as opposed to taking some risks and living in some new ways.

This is not to suggest that every one of us has some powerful artistic ability waiting to be released. Well, perhaps we do, but it is not the case that everyone who decides to change their lives to explore painting or writing is necessarily very good at what they set out to do. Perhaps that is not the point: rather, by exploring their creative skills, everyone is finding out more about themselves, whether or not the outcome is satisfying to others. I am suggesting that artists help us along the path of the examined life, by allowing us to explore ideas, images and feelings that might otherwise be left unstudied and unrealised. The arts can be one part of the environment that encourage us to try something new, and even to become different.

It can be a challenging path, to try to do something different. Friends can look at you askance, and say "you're going to do what?" How lucky is it when we meet someone who supports our tentative endeavours at creativity, who sees what we are trying to do, and gives us the advice we need to make the steps firmer and clearer.

Of course, all this discussion presumes a degree of freedom of choice that we may not feel we have, and we may need to be reminded about the conclusions we drew in that earlier discussion of organisations that took place in Chapter 2. It is a fact that organisations require largely conventional behaviour. The only way to coordinate the activities of large numbers of people is to have rules, roles and requirements that do not allow flexibility and creativity. I am actually quite happy about that. When I fly in a modern aeroplane, I am reassured to know that the plane has been built to very exacting standards, carefully quality controlled, and that the pilots have been trained and are required to undertake regular re-accreditation. When I go in to a hospital, I am reassured that the doctors have been carefully trained and their capabilities monitored by an external accrediting organisation. I don't want creative aeroplane builders, or surgeons who decide to abandon the carefully developed procedures of their profession.

Ah, but I do want change. In fact, I want an even safer aeroplane in the future. I want to be reassured that my pilot has not only met the training needs, but also is not tired, drunk or depressed. As for going in to hospital, of course it is the case that I want the drugs, the treatments and the practices to be continually improved. I want creativity on top of conformity!! I also look for change in areas where procedures and requirements are not as strong as I would like them: every time I drive my car and see a 'near miss' I wish that the same exacting standards and safety procedures could be put into motor car travel as exist in aircraft travel. This is where creativity is important. My hope is for some 'safe' non-conformity, someone inventing a new anti-collision system, or even cleverly re-examining how we manage travel and safety.

As a teacher of business students, I find this balance between confidence in following the rules versus a desire for innovation and improvement poses an interesting dilemma. I know that organisational practice needs to be understood. On the other hand, as I happen to be interested in creativity and innovation, I want those same students to 'think out of the box', and come up with new, better and alternative ways of doing things. In order to strike the right balance between ensuring things are done well and new ideas are pursued, we spend time talking about such strange places as "skunk works" (backrooms areas where a few innovative souls can work on new ideas, but are kept away from the ordinary production processes) and "ambidextrous organisations" (where there are carefully designed mechanisms to help transfer new ideas into effective future practice).

As you can see from these terms, the very language of innovation in organisations is revealing. We often find ourselves discussing how to manage the trade-off between conformity (and eventual business failure as innovative competitors develop better products and services), and unacceptably high levels of risk (when innovation takes over, and the business does not pay enough attention to maintaining its present activities, thereby losing customers and income). The very words 'risk' and 'failure' point to the need to contain innovative activity, to keep it out of sight in that aptly named "skunk works". What we are doing, of course, is making sure we manage the innovation process itself – thereby keeping risk under control, but at the same time putting a new kind of conformity in to place.

As we examine the processes of innovation, it turns out that the trade-off between conformity and innovation looks different for different kinds of organisation. It seems that for mature, well-established organisations, the level of creativity and innovation that occurs is always relatively low. The focus is on incremental improvement, continuous enhancement, rather than big and disruptive changes. Why is this? It seems that such companies find that that it is easier, and still financially rewarding, to improve on what they have done in the past, than try to invent something truly new. Indeed, as such organisations find their markets becoming more mature and failing to grow, then the emphasis tends to shift to rethinking how to deliver the business, still seeing this as preferable to trying to develop entirely new products or services.

However, really disruptive or innovative ideas are far more common in smaller companies and start-ups. They are able to live with the risky nature of new ideas in the sense that many of these new companies fail, or never begin to grow – the innovation, or those managing it, just don't manage to create sustainable businesses. However, those that do survive those difficult first years then go on to create the next group of larger organisations (often, as they grow, taking over their less agile predecessors who have been focussing, of necessity, on small scale improvement).

All this speaks to the theme at the beginning of this chapter – our fascination with pushing the boundaries, doing something new, the eccentric artist or innovator, and our worries about stepping too far out of line. Organisations are revealing, as Socrates argued, because they may demonstrate in an obvious way issues that are also important to the individual. What can we learn from looking at organisations and innovation? How can this be applied back to ourselves, not necessarily as would-be artists (though you may be one), but as people seeking to understand themselves better and willing to be open to change?

One theme that may be useful is to look at the language that is used. In organisations, discussions about innovation often are couched in terms of 'taking risks' and the likelihood of 'failure'. There are often processes put in place to 'check the probability of success' and 'filter out less promising ideas'. The uses of words do shape our responses. If we were to replace 'risk' with 'experiment' how different that suddenly seems. Experiments are the stuff of life, tentatively testing ideas and actions out to see what response occurs. Isn't that what many artists have done – experimented with colour, sound, shape, image, idea, to see where it leads: you only need to look at some artists notebooks to see the wealth of experimentation that takes place.

Similarly, if we were to replace 'failure' with 'learning', then we can reconceptualise what it means in taking a risk – now renamed 'undertaking an experiment'. In order to learn, you have to do things, often very new things, and then examine the experience of that new path, the consequences, and build a new approach, rethink a direction. We spent a lot of our childhood learning: perhaps we should recognise that life is a never-ending exercise in learning. We were very curious when we were young, so surely active curiosity should still be part of our lives. "Active curiosity?" By that I mean that we do not wait to be told things, but go out to find out for ourselves.

Perhaps the best example I can give is being a tourist in a new place: new places are experiments that have already been created for you to explore. One way to be a tourist is to read the guidebook and, camera in hand, go and look at the things you are told to see. Yes, there is that building, that church, and yes; inside there is a curious sculpture on the west wall. Record what you were told to find, and feel that you have seen something new. The alternative is to go to interesting places (guidebooks do have their place) and then simply look around, and ask yourself why this is the case as you try and sort out the odd juxtapositions within another city or another church. Sit and look, and begin to see things, and keep asking 'what is this about?' 'why did this happen?', and especially 'what does this mean?' I am still trying to sort out why pulpits in churches migrate from one side of the nave to the other: is it decision made by church architects, a result of different faith traditions, or just the practice of different centuries? Active curiosity is about questioning things for yourself. Guidebooks, like this one, can help you find where there are questions worth asking, but only you can formulate the questions that make sense to you, that help you learn.

That brings us back to those artists we first mentioned at the start of this chapter. Do artists expect us to be passive recipients of what they have done? Homer told the story of the Iliad in order for people to think and talk about so many things – about war, about love, about the nature of society in Greek times, about the role of the gods – the list goes on, and the story is a rich source of ideas and topics for discussion. It was also oral history, and at that time the only way to ensure that history was remembered. Francis Ford Coppola made a film about Vietnam to present an alternative view of what was happening there, and to provoke discussion and disagreement. The film is not just about the horrors of war, and the ethics of how modern war is conducted. He also wanted us to think about how we see ourselves, and did so through the confrontation between Major Willard, going up the Mekong River, and the bloated figure of a man gone native. What had happened? Was this about something that could happen to anyone who 'goes native'?

In an interesting way, art is often successful when it encourages us to talk to other people. When Greek audiences listened to Homer, they talked about what had happened, about the role of the gods in the story and in their lives, about the nature of heroism and the importance of family and friends. Often people coming out of the cinema want to discuss what they have just seen – not merely in saying that was a 'great film', but in exploring some of the issues that were addressed. It is a tentative thing, challenging our self-confidence and our desire to learn. In some ways we want to cling on to our perception of what took place and not be proven wrong, trying to avoid hearing points of view with which we disagree or which might upset our own. At the same time, we want to hear what others have to say, to debate and explore. Art has both a personal dimension and a public one.

Through their creative endeavours artists can prod, poke and push us to recognise that we do not have to remain passive, stuck in our routines, accepting the world around us. We, too, can be inquisitive, we can change things, and we can be different from the way we are today. The changes we make can be small, but can help us see ourselves in a different light. The businessman who takes up carpentry at night appreciates timbers and the possibilities of shape and form. He learns about tools and techniques, and when he travels takes a delight in seeing what wood carvers have done because he now appreciates both their skills and their intent.

To allow ourselves to be creative – in writing, cooking or taking photographs, in any medium – is to give ourselves the privilege of being more than well behaved and conventional. More than this, in whatever way to try to explore that innovative side of our character, it gives us another reflection back on our selves: on who we are, and what we might be. Artists may often be mad, bad and dangerous, but precisely because they are, they give us licence to learn a bit more about ourselves.

Field Guide Criterion 6:
Expression: Conformity versus Creativity

Appreciating the passions of others is a function of our willingness to step outside the comfortable routines that define our daily lives, and being really willing to engage with other ways of living. The arts push this alternative to us in a clear and uncompromising way: this is not about the hackneyed picture of being a bohemian, living in garret, and indulging in the excesses of life. It is about exploring new ways of seeing the world, and being able to present them to others. In all the recent discussions about city dwellers wanting to return to a simpler environment, there is less exploration of the opportunities this presents outside of living a rural life, re-engaging with real communities, and eating healthy food again. Surely the opportunity is to be different, and to explore aspects of our selves that otherwise will remain buried under respectability and convention.

Is this a criterion for the field guide? I think there is a dimension in our lives which is about expression, which we can define as a continuum between leading a conventional life, and being a good citizen by conforming to the expectations of others, and being a creative person, living on the edge, always trying to upset conventions and seeing things anew. This seems to be about our ways of expressing ourselves, defined by a continuum that ranges between conformity and creativity, and one where we might seek to find the appropriate balance between routine and significant change.

The questions to be explored here are about how you want to express yourself:

- How do you see your everyday life – as one where you are good at meeting expectations and obligations, a life of conventional good citizenship?
- Are there areas in which you would like to explore some other facets of your character?
- Do you want to escape a conventional life and be a radical, a creator, a rethinker?
- Is there a place between these two extremes that would seem to be the place you seek?

7

Trying to be consistent

In this chapter the focus is on perception, on the way in which we look at our lives, on how we make sense of things. There is a very interesting contrast to be drawn here, which is between being open-minded – willing to accept and live with a whole variety of ways of perceiving what is happening, even when these different ways contain elements are sometimes confusing or even contradictory; and being ideological – seeing things through a specific framework, an explicit and coherent way of making sense of the world.

As with many words in this book, definitions are important, and the word 'ideology' often means different things for different people. When I use the word ideology, I am talking about a way of looking the world around us, a framework for making sense, a lens or a perspective that is often broad in what it covers. What does that mean? Perhaps an example might be helpful. One ideology with which we are quite familiar is a Christian ideology. Another is the 'free market capitalism' view of the world. In both these cases, we are talking about a view of the world that includes a more or less coherent set of principles, theories and value statements, a whole framework for understanding.

In the Christian ideology, there is a theory about people, their souls, their relationship to God, and the concept of resurrection. There is a whole set of principles embodied in The Ten Commandments, and yet further principles laid out in the teachings of Jesus; there are values about love, charity, respect, and so much more. It is an encompassing, broad framework that shapes a Christian's view of the world in which he or she lives. In the same way, a free market capitalist has a set of theories about how the world works, focussed around the ideas of the operations and hidden hand of the market; principles about reward for effort, and the effectiveness of the laws of supply and demand; there are values to do with honesty, integrity, contractual obligations and so on. It, too, is a way of making sense of how we live in the world, and equally important for many people. As these two examples make clear, ideologies are pervasive – they become embedded in many aspects of our lives – and they often sit 'behind' the things we do and talk about on an everyday basis. There are many other ideologies – Marxism, Feminism, Humanism, Islam, and so the list goes on. Although I have described them as being very broad, it is sometimes the case that we can hold more than one ideology together in our heads, managing to ignore or avoid areas of contradiction.

What is the ideology that sits behind your way of looking at the world? That is not an easy question to answer, and perhaps we should start with an approach Socrates favoured, and begin with asking a simpler question, which is: What are the principles that we find important? If we can identify these, then we may be able to move on to look at how these are a constituent part of our ideological framework.

We used an example earlier in this book where a manager, on being promoted, had to choose between two candidates to replace him in his former position: the loyal and able worker, or the relatively new and brilliant recruit. When this was discussed early on it was presented as a choice between applying one principle or not: should we reward loyalty or ignore it?

Of course, that was a very simplistic presentation. A better way of viewing this situation might have been to say there were a number of conflicting principles at stake here:

- One principle is loyalty: "we should reward loyalty"
- A second principle might be merit: "we should reward talent"
- Another is equality: "treat everyone in the same way"
- Yet another is compliance: "follow the rules of the organisation"

- Yet one other is utilitarianism: "act in such a way that you maximise the benefits for the greatest number of people"
- Another is authenticity: "you must be true to yourself"

I am sure there are many others, but those will do for a start. Now we can see that – as is usually the case in real life – the central problem here is trying to answer the question 'how do we resolve the contradictions between a number of seemingly equally important principles or rules?' We identified two approaches earlier: either you determine that one principle has priority over all the others; or you try to balance out the competing principles, and identify the approach that best meets most of them.

An example of the first of these approaches, that one principle that has priority over all the others, (the 'transcendent' principle), might be the so-called golden rule, which is usually stated as: "do unto others as you would have them do to you". Actually, Confucius, who was one of the earliest to express this view, put it the other way round: 'do not do unto others what you would not have them do unto you'. The difference between the two is important. In the usually expressed form the injunction is positive, and at the same time very open-ended. In the Confucian form, the injunction is negative, and prohibits an action – and in that sense is much clearer.

How would we apply the principle set out in the golden rule to the situation above? First, as the manager, you might observe that the organisation has rules for considering people for jobs, and you want these to continue to be applied to yourself and others. You know that one of these rules is that 'the best qualified person will be the one selected for the job'. On that basis you would recommend that the newer but more brilliant staff member to be appointed …… wouldn't you? If you start treating some people in one way and others in another, then you have abandoned the golden rule, and there will be no consistency in the way things are done.

Actually, it is possible to construct some other ways of using the golden rule to resolve this situation that would lead to quite a different conclusion. For example, you might have observed that although there are rules about appointing staff, in practice choices are often made on loyalty. As far as you can see, this is why you were appointed to your new position. Isn't this the way the company works in practice, rewarding loyalty. Applying the golden rule to that construction of the situation would suggest you should promote the loyal staff member. Oh dear – it seems that applying a single principle isn't as easy as we were hoping! Even in this simple case, it is evident that applying the golden rule may take us beyond considering yourself and another person on to considering broader organisations rules and practices.

What we are discussing here is one form of theoretical reasoning. It is a form of argument that examines the principles at stake, and seeks to resolve in abstract terms how they should be applied. This first approach, which is often used, is where we identify whatever is the most important principle or overall reason for choice of an action, and then argue that the other principles are interesting, important even, but subordinate.

The other form of theoretical reasoning is not to claim one principle supersedes all others, but to try to find a way of linking the various principles together, and identifying a logical outcome. I can imagine arguing that it is important to reward loyalty; that this is the way that we treat everyone in practice, even though it is not strictly following the explicit rules of the organisation which require making appointments on the basis of merit; that this would benefit the organisation most because loyalty is what makes the place work; and, hopefully, it is fairly close to being true to myself. Everything tells me I should be doing this, even though it does go against our formal organisational procedures.

Either form of theoretical reasoning uses logic to determine a reasoned conclusion. However, as can be seen in our simple case, even then the actual reasoning can become quite complex.

There is an alternative to theoretical reasoning, and this is to use practical reasoning. Central to practical reasoning are the concepts of 'circumstances' and 'precedent' – looking at what others have decided in similar situations. Circumstances are the particular facts of the case, which are often unique. Precedents are previous decisions that have been made about the same or similar situations. Taking circumstances and precedents together means that we can draw on the reasoning of others, but at the same time allow for the distinctive circumstances that characterise this situation. Precedent and circumstances mediate the application of the principles. In the situation we were describing earlier, the actions of the manager's manager would set a precedent as to what approach should be taken. Our fears about being passed over by other more able people might be one of the circumstances we would consider – perhaps the newer recruit had already made it clear she was after the manager's job.

The use of either theoretical or practical reasoning represents alternative ways of applying principles. Why is this important in thinking about ideologies? Well, we defined ideologies as including a number of principles. In some cases, there may be one among these that has precedence over all the others, but in most cases we would expect that the bundle of principles within an ideology may lead us to use theoretical or practical reasoning to determine what to do.

We can take the Christian framework as an example to illustrate this. Some would argue that the golden rule has a unique place within Christianity, in which case this would always be the touchstone against which to make decisions. I am not sure if that is the case, and it does seem likely to me that Christian ideology is more like those situations where there are a number of principles, some clear and independent, and some overlapping and potentially competing with one another: the meek shall inherit the earth, the last will come first, worldly success is not the path to salvation; at the same time we must use the talents we have been given to our best ability, and we will be rewarded accordingly – whether we have ten talents or only one. Consider these competing ideas: should we work hard – and therefore be seen as successful – or not? This is the kind of issue with which the church has wrestled over a long period of time.

In practical reasoning, we look for those precedents that help us make difficult decisions, but we also have to look to ourselves, and the values and circumstances, that we see as important in each particular problem we try to resolve. Some centuries ago, practical reasoning was called casuistry and it was seen as an important skill. In the Roman Catholic Church there were learned debates about what to do in particular circumstances, trying to determine rules to show how practical issues could be resolved. However, the approach fell out of favour, as the debates were seen as becoming abstract and esoteric, rather than focussed on being helpful. It was seen as another example of abstruse theological analysis, of trying to work out "how many angels can stand on the head of a pin". The desire to set precedents began to overtake the value of assessing grounds for decision making. However, in today's complex world where most moral issues are not easily resolved by simply applying one or more basic principles, the casuist's concern with practical reasoning seems well placed. As we have argued throughout this book, practical reasoning is a helpful technique.

When we were exploring how to deal with principles in making decisions, we observed that one approach was to identify the most important one. This is based on the assumption that it *is* possible to find a principle that is absolute and which is prior to any others, a transcendent principle, or what Kant was to call a 'categorical imperative'. In this case, we have to face an important question – where do we find this prior or absolute principle? We have discussed a couple of examples before – Bentham's utilitarianism, and Confucius and the golden rule. Thus the question becomes a concern with the source of a principle, and how we know that this should be given priority or precedence over any others. It seems a little weak to argue "because Bentham – or Confucius – said so". ; We seek something we can agree is an ultimate authority, rather than the views of an individual – however clever that person might be.

One source of fundamental or overarching principles is through revelation – that is to say, through the belief that these principles exist independently of the normal sphere of human endeavour, and are there to be discovered. For those of us within a religious tradition, the principle source of revelation has been the words of a prophet or a text that has divine authority: Jesus or the Holy Bible for Christians, for example, or Mohammed and the Q'ran for Muslims. The value of revelation is that the source is incontrovertible – it is 'beyond our understanding' – and if you accept the source, then the revelatory rules cannot be ignored. As I am sure you have realised, the other advantage of the revelation is that it gives you a complete ideological framework: the only challenges that remain are in applying the ideology to practice.

Actually, revelation in practice can turns out to be quite hard work. The Holy Bible, as an example, is full of suggested rules and principles (including the Ten Commandments, and many of Jesus' prescriptions and admonitions). However, while some are clear and unambiguous – like the Ten Commandments – others are less definitive. In this situation we often turn to theologians to explain to us what is meant by what has been said – a process that is as familiar to us in the Christian tradition as turning to Rabbis in the Jewish tradition, or Imams in the Islamic tradition. Those wise theologians interpret for us, translating what was said to allow us to understand what lay beneath the words. An exception would be those religious traditions that say that all the writings are to be taken literally, at face value.

There are other 'religious' frameworks, of course. Buddhist adherents believe that revelation does not come from the study of texts or the words of a leader (even though Buddha is a crucial thinker in the Buddhist belief framework), but rather through meditation, through suspending involvement in the press of activities in the world, and reaching deep internally. Such religious traditions emphasise that understanding (and hence values) are to be found within, rather than documented in one way or another. Prophets become guides, showing us the way to find true knowledge for ourselves: how to live, and how to find balance and peace, and how to achieve salvation.

Other sources of overarching or prior values may to come from appealing to logic. Utilitarianism is of this kind: it does seem reasonable to argue that if you are going to make a choice, the better choice will always be the one that impacts badly on the smallest number of people, and that brings the most benefit to the largest. Somehow, this has the ring of being "the worst form of decision making, except for all those other forms that have been tried" (actually, it was Winston Churchill who said something like that, but his quote was "democracy is the worst form of government, except for all those other forms that have been tried"!!).

I suspect the golden rule is also like this: if you want one principle to live by, then reciprocity seems a good starting point. Certainly, Confucius was a very practical person: many of the things he said in The Analects seem to be based on the principle that society works well because we have all agreed to follow the rules, and that the role of the leader is to make sure that those rules are clearly understood and adopted.

However, some of us have one concern when we are reading Confucius – or Bentham – or anyone else who comes up with that overarching (or transcendent) rule, and this is that their principles can seem very closed. Surely as time goes by, we learn more, and can develop better ways of doing things. Just as Winston Churchill would not be greatly impressed by democracy as it is practiced today (and disappointed we have not developed something better yet), so I believe that we should keep on searching for a better basis on which we should live. This is one of the reasons John Rawls is held in such high esteem – he really sought to develop principles that were universal and yet which reflected what we had come to understand in the 20th Century, to take us a step forward.

To have one principle that stands above all others is an extreme position, of course. If you believe this should be the case, then it is important you explore how this principle will relate to practice: how it is to be interpreted, and how other – subordinate – principles should then serve to modify or elaborate how that superior principle.

For many of us, that is an ideal that is too hard to apply in practice, and we tend to support the approach where there are several key principles, and we have to apply practical reasoning to determine what to do in particular circumstances. However, we are still left with the challenge of finding the source of these principles. Then again, Socrates never claimed that leading the 'examined life' was going to be easy! Indeed, he would be happy with the thought that we have to work hard to justify why we believe a particular principle or rule is appropriate, and carry out a thorough examination as to suitability of what we are proposing.

Practical reasoning is tough work in that it insists on circumstances and competing principles to be assessed, and then justifying why one element of a situation is given precedence over another. One of my favourite case studies is about testing a new drug on children – it is based on a real life situation in which an opportunity arose to test a new drug on children living in an underdeveloped country where an epidemic was raging. The drug had been approved for testing on children in the USA, but the number of children who suited the testing requirements was limited. The outbreak of an epidemic overseas seemed to offer an unexpected but needed chance to extend the testing. A utilitarian would have little doubt about situations of this kind: unfortunate, but as we need to test drugs in order to find new treatments for illnesses, we have to take the opportunity to test where we can. If some drugs do not work out, the testing was for the benefit of us all, albeit at the cost of a just a few people. Those of us who are not utilitarian try to grapple with all sorts of issues in a case like this. Was it fair to go to an underdeveloped country where medical services were limited? Did people understand what was being proposed? Were the rules of testing followed rigorously? Oddly, in discussing cases like this, we often end up supporting the utilitarian argument. That seems to be the corollary of living in a world where progress is seen as a paramount aim.

All this discussion has focussed on one extreme, where we have a set of principles, an ideology, which is the basis we use to determine how we act. Is there another extreme? The opposite would seem to be unreflective action. What does that mean? Well, I think that in many areas of our lives, we just get on and do things without spending much – or any – time in reflection. Working in a factory, selling goods in a store, there are many occasions when others have set the agenda, and we simply do as we are bid. Much of the time, this is unproblematic – someone else has done the hard work of planning, and we are simply executing the tasks that are required. However, we do know that in extreme cases this can lead to awful or immoral behaviour – guards shepherding people into gas chambers – and ultimate ends like that should be a warning to us. Are we sometimes guilty of doing things when we should be thinking carefully about the consequences of our actions? Isn't this just what Socrates was asking us to address?

One example of unreflective action is acting without examining what we are doing. Another is when we are so comfortable with a set of values and principles, an ideology as I have described it, that we see no reason to question its basis. For example, if you are a strong believer in the value of the free and open market, then you will be able to get on in business by following the principles that such a perspective entails. Your task in the marketplace is to produce the goods or services that you wish to sell, and to find customers who are willing to pay the price that you want. That price is influenced by a number of criteria: in basic terms these might include the prices you have to pay for 'inputs' such as raw materials, labour, know-how, etc.; the scarcity of the resource that you are offering; the level of need that exists in the marketplace; and the competitive environment. Some times your expectations are met, and sometimes not: the market is often 'fickle'. However, you understand the logic, and you continue to seek customers for the goods you produce, at a price that allows you to stay in business. You have accepted a particular framework of ideas, an ideology, and spend little or no time at all in reflection; no reason to question its basis.

If someone is said to be 'ideological' today, it is often associated with extremism of one kind or another. However, ideologies are not owned by Marxists, terrorists or fanatics. Ideologies are simply coherent bodies of ideas that we can accept or reject: once accepted, ideologies often seem to move into the background, becoming another element of that 'taken for granted' world that we have discussed before. Ideologies become 'right' for us because that is the way the world is as we see it, and for that very reason, when people with different ideologies confront one another, they almost always have great difficulty in understanding each other. Their coherent sets of ideas are pervasive (they run through everything), and embedded (they are deeply held, and not easily brought to the surface to be questioned).

We considered another perspective on the frameworks used to make sense of things when we talked about scientists in Chapter 5. There we noted that scientists sometimes use the word 'paradigm' to describe this phenomenon, rather than talking about ideologies. In fact, their analyses of paradigms in science can help us understand the importance of ideologies. To use an example, take the different paradigms of astronomy over the centuries. For a long time, everyone believed that the earth was the centre of the universes, and everything revolved around the earth. Belief in that paradigm meant that there had to be some very convoluted theories developed to explain some observable phenomena, like the paths followed by a number of the planets. Despite this, the model held firm: after all, it is not a surprising view of the world if you feel that the human race is special, and so it and where it lives must be at the centre of the universe.

Eventually that paradigm was questioned, and a new one put in place – the earth revolves around the sun. This immediately provided a basis to address a number of the anomalies that had been 'explained away' under the earlier paradigm. However, the new paradigm raised a new set of questions, and a new set of anomalies began to emerge. Of these one of the most important was – how did the earth and the sun get there? Bigger theories were developed, and in time this led to two competing paradigms – the steady state universe, in which the universe is constantly creating matter, new galaxies and solar systems coming in to being; and the 'big bang' theory, in which the whole universe was 'created' at a particular point in time, and has been evolving and expanding ever since. Now the big bang paradigm is held to be correct. I am sure there are anomalies that this paradigm has yet to explain, and in time they will be covered in yet another more inclusive theory. At the same time, of course, this paradigm creates some other questions – like 'what was there before the big bang?" For those who ask, it may not be very consoling to be told that this is a meaningless question.

The scientists' view of paradigms helps us look more closely at ideologies. They are both terms that refer to relatively closed and internally fairly coherent systems. At the same time, they usually presume some fundamental questions that cannot be answered, or they skate over some facts or observations that do not seem to fit. These questions or anomalies are very important, as they are usually the points at which – eventually – an alternative view gains some traction. However, most of the time, most of us just accept the view of the world with which they have become comfortable, and those anomalies and questions (like those in a scientific paradigm) remain ignored or invisible.

Some people like to believe that they are free of the world of ideologies and complicating theories. They are open-minded, and get on and deal with the realities of life, constantly "rubbing up against the world of hard facts and intractable data". If there is one writer who has given me particular pleasure in this regard, it has to be Machiavelli. Though his written style is now a little hard to follow, and though his examples draw on knowledge of antiquity that I certainly do not possess, nonetheless he is a provocative and confronting writer. Every time I go back to Machiavelli, I am rewarded with writing that really makes me think – often in disagreement, but never without interest and attention.

Machiavelli has had bad press. Many people are 're-written' by history, and Machiavelli has to be a prime example. We use the word 'Machiavellian' to describe actions "marked by cunning, duplicity, or bad faith" (Merriam Webster, 2010). However, when we go back and read his classic work The Prince we discover the story is far from black and white.

Machiavelli saw himself as an observer, an empiricist, and he sought to identify what should be done if you wished to become a Prince, and hold on to your power. He drew his conclusions by looking at the practice of successful and unsuccessful kings and princes, not by developing an abstract theory. In some ways he reminds us of Glaucon, (whom we quoted in Chapter 2), and Machiavelli was the writer quoted then who summarised his perceptions of men as being "ungrateful, voluble, dissemblers, anxious to avoid danger, and covetous of gain". Indeed, Machiavelli also shares Glaucon's view that it is simply foolish to be good all the time:

> *"But my intention being to write something of use to those who understand, it appears to me more proper to go to the real truth of the matter than to its imagination; and many have imagined republics and principalities which have never been seen or known to exist in reality; for how we live is so far removed from how we ought to live, that he who abandons what is done for what ought to be done, will rather learn to bring about his own ruin than his*

preservation. A man who wishes to make a profession of goodness in everything must necessarily come to grief among so many who are not good. Therefore it is necessary for a prince, who wishes to maintain himself, to learn how not to be good, and to use this knowledge and not use it, according to the necessity of the case."
(Machiavelli, The Prince, Section 15)

In setting out to identify this 'real truth of the matter' Machiavelli poses a number of puzzles that we need to address if we are going to 'maintain ourselves' – by which he means hold on to our power. He has an open-minded approach to these puzzles, and is willing to find answers by simply looking at what has worked in practice.

For example, Machiavelli asks the question "how we to be regarded?" Perhaps we would like to be seen as good, and Machiavelli suggests one of the criteria of being good is to be seen as being liberal and generous. He observes that being generous can actually be very risky. Suppose you want to be seen in this way, and decide to give everyone something more (perhaps by increasing their salaries). People are happy you have done this. Next year, to show you are really generous, you increase wages again. Now you have created an expectation – as a generous boss, you will always be increasing salaries every year. However, these increased wages are proving to be a significantly added cost to your enterprise, and so you have to look for ways to offset this increased expenditure. Perhaps you raise the prices of the goods or services you provide: this leads customers to begin to look for alternatives, and you begin to lose business – and now the burden of generosity becomes greater, to the point that you can only survive by cutting costs, especially salaries. Or perhaps you ask people to work harder, and what seemed to be generosity comes to be seen more as a bribe. Now you are no longer seen so much as generous but rather as exploitative. Machiavelli concludes that the best approach is to be miserly, in this case this would mean that you would hardly increase wages at all, but continue to run your business well: by this means, profits increase and, eventually, when others are in trouble your staff look and realise that you were looking after their interests: that you were a good boss after all!

In another example, he considers what to do if there are some ineffective or disloyal people in the organisation. He suggests that you should act decisively and early, and get rid of these people before they cause trouble and lead to longer term instabilities. He also says, in effect, that you should 'do it once, do it quickly, and then you won't need to continue sacking staff'. In that way you will gain a reputation of being tough, but fair. The alternative path is to keep on looking for troublemakers, and sack them every so often. That will create a climate of fear, and one in which people will be de-motivated, and you will always be standing "knife in hand" waiting to get rid of the next person, and at the same time fearful, trying to avoid any blow that might be struck in your direction.

Machiavelli demands our attention because his observations make good sense. We can all think of a manager we have known who was constantly 'stabbing people in the back' and that no one trusted as a result. We can all remember the 'generous boss' who used to pay a bonus every year, and then suddenly stopped because it was no longer convenient to do so – even though we worked even harder that year.

Is Machiavelli a true empiricist, just looking at 'the facts'? Today, with the benefit of hindsight and analysis, we can say 'no!' Machiavelli had a number of implicit theories in his head when he went off to look at history. He believed power was effective when it was exercised in an unfettered way. What did he think of the power and leadership of someone like Jesus, who didn't fit that image? We don't know, because in Machiavelli's analysis of leaders, Jesus as a leader doesn't get a mention (an interesting omission, since Machiavelli was both a moral person and a Christian believer).

In the same way, Machiavelli would have a great deal of difficulty making sense of the writings of Robert Greenleaf on 'servant leadership' (Greenleaf, 1970), or Jim Collins on 'level 5 leadership' (Collins, 2001), largely because he would not see such approaches as these as being about leadership at all. Thus Machiavelli had his embedded ideologies, too.

We have to be careful when identifying particular characteristics of an ideology. To have a point of view does not mean that your approach is of no value. In fact, it is just the opposite. Once we acknowledge Machiavelli's perspective on the world, then his contribution is enhanced, rather than reduced. He is a wonderful analyst of people who believe in power and control, and he still offers so many insights into the behaviour of chief executives in companies. I have often thought that The Prince should be renamed The CEO, and with a few changes - replacing the word Prince with CEO, poisoning with outplacement, stabbing with lateral transfer – then it becomes a perceptive guide to the practices and preferences of many 20th century businessmen. What Machiavelli saw applies to many today who see their role as being about seizing and keeping power, whose own ideologies are about power and control: he is of less help when we want to rethink the company and the practice of business in the 21st Century.

The Prince remains one of the great books of western literature. Beautifully written, even if at first reading the text can seem a little complex to follow at times, it repays careful study. It gives innumerable insights into the world of power politics and domination, and its application goes beyond the management of the state to address some of the issues facing contemporary businesses and organisations, and even the ways in which families operate. It is a carefully examined view of life, and if it is not about how the 'good life' might be constructed in the 21st Century, it contains much to make us think and ponder.

I like to contrast Machiavelli with a contemporary writer on leadership, Ronald Heifetz. Looking at leadership through the eyes of someone concerned with the public sector, Heifetz has a very different image of what a leader does. In Leadership without easy answers (1994), Heifetz puts forward an alternative view of what is important in leadership. Instead of focussing on power and control, he argues that the challenges that leaders face today are what he calls 'adaptive': the task of the leader is to assist and enable people to deal with change and its consequences. In one of his commentaries, he goes on to argue that a key element of this is changing actual behaviour, and that this is hard for many leaders. He suggests that this is because – as we have explored before – changing behaviour requires abandoning embedded and long-standing patterns, the very behaviours that have probably helped these leaders move up in an organisation. However, if real change is to take place, it has to be across the organisation, and leaders have to enable this.

Heifetz also argues there is another issue here. Adaptive change, changing behaviours in relation to the changes taking place around you, is emotionally threatening. Staff in organisations tend to expect that the leadership will deal with external challenges, and their role is just to get on and do the work. However, a leader today, he suggests, has to help staff see where the problems lie, feel some of the pressure for change, so that they will respond to the need to adapt. He suggests that "Instead of orienting people to their current roles, leaders must disorient them so that new relationships can develop. Instead of quelling conflict, leaders have to draw the issues out. Instead of maintaining norms, leaders have to challenge "the way we do business" and help others distinguish immutable values from historical practices that must go." (Heifetz and Laurie, 2001, p 3). What a shift in ideology! We have moved from the idea that leadership is about power and control to leadership that is about enabling and support.

Debates over leadership are at the heart of discussions about theory and practice. Much of leadership is simply 'doing what you have learnt works', and there is an implicit ideology about people (about human nature) and about leadership (power and control) that goes unquestioned. However, newer leadership theories change the assumptions. The challenge for the manager today is to come to terms with those assumptions, not just the recommended practice. It continues to be the case that we do not have one theory of leadership that 'works', a transcendental theory, as it were. Rather leadership is always going to be in that hinterland between strong theories – ideological, and limited – and practical decision-making – concerned with practical reasoning and responding to circumstance.

We do not often use the word leadership when talking about families. When Heifetz talks about 'adaptive' leadership I think it makes a great deal of sense when you apply it to the personal realm, as well as to organisations. This was brought home to me one day when I was talking about leadership to a group of managers. They were comfortable with the model they knew well – 'command and control'.

When I tried to explain an alternative approach, I suddenly thought of family life, and the challenges of exercising leadership with your partner or children. That helped the managers and it helped me, too. We are not as unfamiliar with alternative theories of leadership as we might think, but we do tend to separate family life and organisational life so sharply that we cannot see the possible connections.

Sometimes ideologists are important because they help explain and justify the way things are today, giving legitimacy to power. John Locke wrote two great treatises on government and economics, in part to demolish the theory of the divine right of kings, and in part to justify the role of the state, and the individual's right to property. His task was to justify and provide a basis for what had become practice. It can be contrasted with the writings of someone like Karl Marx; a theoretician who wrote to establish what should be done in the future. Marx was concerned with writing a justification for change, an ideology that has been so important in the history of the 20th Century.

History reminds us that a lot of change has taken place through leaders pursuing ideologies, and the combination of strong leadership (in Machiavelli's terms) and a strong ideology can be both very effective, but also can be very dangerous: ideology has its blind-side. Lenin, Trotsky and the other leaders of the Russian Revolution had read their Marx and Engels, and applied the theory without doubts. They had been told:

> "We have seen above that the first step in the revolution by the working class is to raise the proletariat to the position of ruling class, to establish democracy.
> The proletariat will use its political supremacy to wrest by degrees all capital from the bourgeoisie, to centralize all instruments of production in the hands of the state, i.e., of the proletariat organized as the ruling class, and to increase the total of productive forces as rapidly as possible.
> Of course, in the beginning this cannot be effected expect by means of despotic inroads on the rights of property and on the conditions of bourgeois production; by means of measures, therefore, which appear economically insufficient and untenable, but which, in the course of the movement outstrip themselves, necessitate further

inroads upon the old social order, and are unavoidable as a means of entirely revolutionizing the mode of production.
These measures will, of course, be different in different countries.
....
When in the course of development class distinctions have disappeared and all production has been concentrated in the hands of a vast association of the whole nation, the public power will lose its political character. Political power, properly so called, is merely the organized power of one class for oppressing another. If the proletariat during its contest with the bourgeoisie is compelled by the force of circumstances to organize itself as a class; if by means of a revolution it makes itself the ruling class and, as such, sweeps away by force the old conditions of production, then it will, along with these conditions, have swept away the conditions for the existence of class antagonisms and of classes generally, and will thereby have abolished its own supremacy as a class.
In place of the old bourgeois society, with its classes and class antagonisms, we shall have an association in which the free development of each is the condition for the free development of all."

(Marx and Engels, 1848)

Somehow, the arguments supporting the causes and the imperatives that would lead to the revolutionary path for change were much clearer than the outcome that revolution would achieve. In the event, what Marx and Engels saw as a path to equality became a path to supremacy for a new group – first the communists, and eventually Stalin and his apparatchiks. Ideological leadership can be blind to consequences, and blind to practical realities.

Of course, it is easy to see this with the benefit of hindsight, just as Machiavelli could offer his practical advice based on the experience of leaders in the preceding centuries. It is much harder the other way round. In Chapter 3 we saw that projecting plans into the future is a hazardous task, given the uncertainty and unpredictability that must always be true about the future. Could Marx and Engels have foreseen the way in which the bourgeoisie would continue to adapt and change in the face of economic and social change? No more easily than we can today, which means very little at all!

Today we recognise that true 'objectivity' is impossible: we see the world through frameworks, ideologies or paradigms, and they are only thrown into disarray when we find ourselves bumping into things out there that refuse to be categorised in our terms. The power of theory rests in its ability to help us make sense of our world. The power of practice is that it tests our theories, by asking them to work in practice.

Is it possible, at the other extreme, to be completely open-minded, and not have to sustain a particular ideology (or set of ideologies)? A truly open-minded person is always willing to be persuaded of a course of action to address a specific issue, even if this is quite contradictory to the approach they might have used previously. A totally open-minded person, devoid of any set of core principles and values, would always be adjusting what they did to the prevailing influences – in other words, a 'flip-flopper'. Neither an ideologue nor a flip-flopper seem to represent very helpful ways of thinking about what is happening.

Field Guide Criterion 7
Perception: Ideological versus Open-minded

One of the less edifying situations today is to observe two people who hold very different points of view, often politicians, debating an issue. As we listen to them speaking, we realize we are seeing ideology at its worst. Each sees and hears things according to the framework they have adopted, and neither is able to find common ground with the other.

This seems to highlight two issues. First, ideologies can become self-fulfilling – to paraphrase from a famous sociological study, the things that we believe real are real in their consequences. Second, it throws into sharp relief the question as to what we mean by 'facts'. Machiavelli had no doubts about the world in which he lived. He observed the history of kings, princes and dictators, and drew his own conclusions: unlike many other writers who are adept at speculating what the world might be like, Machiavelli saw himself as a clear eyed empiricist. Today we tend to view his approach as rather less open-minded, as an example of a mixture of ideology and practice

One step away from being a one-eyed ideologue is to engage in reasoning about the way things are. In looking at the relationship between theoretical and practical reasoning, our concern has been with the extent to which reliance on prior principles – and then the application of logic – can resolve situations, and is something on which we should rely, or how far we have to be circumstantial, taking in to account the competing and conflicting realities in a situation, and making a judgement about what is the best – the most reasonable – approach to adopt.

Given this, the seventh criterion in our field guide is concerned with perception, and with finding the appropriate balance between the extremes of ideology and open-mindedness. At the ideological extreme, we can act without thinking; at the open-minded extreme we can fall into the trap of simply taking up whatever the next person says. The middle ground here is particularly important, where we have to work out how to reason and be open to our biases and frameworks, while still holding to the principles we feel are important.

There is a sequence of questions you might like to explore:

- What are the principles and values that you feel are central to your perception of the world and your place in it?
- How clear are you about the underlying ideologies that support these principles and values?
- How do you deal with situations where principles or values seem to come into conflict?
- How open-minded do you feel you are, and willing to listen to different points of view?
- What are the circumstances in which you feel comfortable in applying logic, and what are those where practical reasoning should apply?
- Do you feel beholden to some theories – some ideologies – and making decisions based on those criteria rather than fully understanding the complexities of real situations?
- Do you feel you have a clear grasp on the facts when you address an issue?
- Are you good at standing back and asking 'why do I think this is the case?'

After exploring all these questions, are there some changes you would like to make in how you look at things – to be clearer about your central principles and values, or to be more open-minded and less constrained in your outlook?

8
In control, out of control

When we talk about change, serious change, we are talking about doing something quite different from the way we have behaved in the past. In order to make such changes, we find we often have to struggle. Part of that struggle is against the inertia of habits and routines, the ways in which we have done things before. Part is against convention, the ways in which others do things. Some times the struggle is against the prevailing laws and regulations. Sometimes the struggle is to uphold the values that you think are important, even though that is not a judgement shared by others.

When someone does something that breaks a habit or a routine, the feedback from others is often cautionary or even disapproving: "That wasn't like you", or "I didn't know you were interested in doing that". Such comments are not helpful. In even the simplest acts of change, we often feel things are moving out of control because we are part of a network of people who expect us – or even require us – to behave in a particular way.

It is for this reason that we sometimes crave a new start, where we are no longer imprisoned by the expectations of others. As parents we know this well with our children – if they slip into routines that hold them back, or lead them to associate with other children we really do not want them to be with, we have to help them find a way to understand the consequences or break free. At the extreme this can be by sending them to a new school, a place where they are able to start over again. The longer we work in a company, the more we get tangled up in relationships and obligations that bind us, and so we look for a new job in the belief that in a new place we will have a new start and do things differently. A new start can be liberating, if we are willing to slough off our old behaviours, and break our previous habits, to somehow regain control over our lives.

Habits are one thing, laws and regulations are another. To break a rule is more public than just breaking a habit, as it touches on our social selves. When this happens, and someone is asked why, the usual response is along the lines of "I did what I was told to do", "I was just following orders", or even "It wasn't my place to question what I had been told". For example, when company staff are investigated over an alleged flouting of the law, (perhaps because of a whistleblower's revelations), then the person concerned will be asked to explain his or her actions. In these cases, it is commonly the case that the person who has been adding illegal chemicals to a product, say, defends himself by explaining that they had been doing what they had been told to do. This was the same answer given by the US marine who was court-martialled over what later became know as the My Lai massacre. His defence was that there was no choice, he was following orders. This touches on a fundamental issue for us – are we in control of our lives, or is it others who control us? A lot of the time, it seems it is social rules, government laws, and all the other instruments of ensuring social conformance. Similarly, if you work for an organisation in any sector of the economy, there are rules, policies, and 'standard operating procedures' that you are expected follow. Some make good sense, especially those concerned with safety, food handling, and other areas where incorrect behaviour can be a source of danger to yourself or others. Others are the culture of the organisation, and more concerned with 'the way things are done around here'.

Sometimes we regard navigating around the rules as acceptable. The accountant who finds a loophole in the tax law is seen to be doing his job, even though the loophole is clearly against the intent of the law. At other times we treat some rules as not so important: a good example are the laws to do with driving speed on the road. These are flouted more than they are observed, as if five miles an hour faster is acceptable and not really breaking the law. Even the young man who drives his car much too fast, is often described as "another youngster with his hormones raging", or we say, "boys will be boys", as if this was sufficient reason, and the behaviour was not really committing a crime. While we seem to allow such excuses, in general to choose to break the rules is to put up with the criticism of others and moral discomfort: to break the law is to be willing to recognise that you have done something that is proscribed, and accept there will be a penalty.

There are times when the breaking of the law becomes central to debates in a country. One of the examples familiar to many of us is when racial segregation was being debated in the USA. One of the key players was Martin Luther King, who advocated civil disobedience in order to make it clear that segregation laws in the USA were wrong. He was very clear about what he was doing, and what he saw as the critical process that needed to be followed before civil disobedience can be a legitimate – if not legal – form of action. In response to a letter from a number of clergy about a number of problems to do with the marches in the South, King replied from jail. It is a beautifully constructed letter, taking each point raised with him in turn and turning it back to the group of clergy by agreeing with the basic argument in each of their points, but challenging their conclusions.

While many of the themes in his reply deserve a chapter of their own, for the purpose of this discussion there is one section that is of particular interest. One of the issues he addressed was to reply to their concern about his support for what they described as 'breaking the law'. King made it clear that to break the law was not an easy choice – that it should only be considered after a number of stages have been undertaken. These included collecting the facts to ensure that there really is a problem with the law and that the problem is one where it is clear that an injustice has occurred. This should be followed by negotiation, to try and resolve the problems that have been identified. If negotiation fails, and if you have gone through a rigorous process of self-examination, being clear about what you want to do and the consequences, then and only then, King argues, can you justifiable take direct action, action that may include knowingly breaking the law. He goes on to say:

> *"I hope you can see the distinction I am trying to point out. In no sense do I advocate evading or defying the law as the rabid segregationist would do. This would lead to anarchy. One who breaks an unjust law must do it openly, lovingly (not hatefully as the white mothers did in New Orleans when they were seen on television screaming "nigger, nigger, nigger"), and with a willingness to accept the penalty. I submit that an individual who breaks a law that conscience tells him is unjust, and willingly accepts the penalty by staying in jail to arouse the conscience of the community over its injustice, is in reality expressing the very highest respect for law."*
>
> (King, 1963, page 2)

King made a critical point about action. If you do not agree with something – on good grounds – you may choose to disobey. To disobey is to break the law, and to do so is to accept – not avoid – the penalty that comes from breaking the law. The act of breaking the law is intended to make it clear that you feel the law is wrong, to highlight that situation, and to arouse concern among others, so there is a move to make changes.

Martin Luther King was trying to deal with those laws that created racial discrimination. He argued that laws that promoted segregation were unjust, and that:

> *"A just law is a manmade code that squares with the moral law or the law of God. An unjust law is a code that is out of harmony with the moral law. To put it in the terms of Saint Thomas Aquinas, an unjust law is a human law that is not rooted in eternal and natural law. Any law that uplifts human personality is just. Any law that degrades human personality is unjust. ..... An unjust law is a code that a majority inflicts on a minority that is not binding on itself. This is difference made legal. On the other hand a just law is a code that a majority compels a minority to follow that it is willing to follow itself. This is sameness made legal .... An unjust law is a code inflicted upon a minority which that minority had no part in enacting or creating because they did not have the unhampered right to vote."*
>
> (King, 1963, page 3)

King's argument is critical. He is saying that we may live in an environment where we believe the rules are wrong, or where the laws are unjust. He identifies three reasons why we might come to the conclusion that a law is unjust – that it does not reflect moral law, or natural law; that it is applied to a minority only; or that a minority was disbarred from discussing and contesting the enactment of that law.

All three of these criteria appear to make sense, but we are particularly interested in the first, because it takes us back to the beginning of this book. King is arguing that a just law is a moral law or natural law. In one sense, we understand this immediately – this is a law that treats us, treats humanity, with respect. In another sense, we are still stuck with the challenge of finding where natural law is written down. I think that King believed that God was a source of natural law: today, many of us would argue that natural law is not to be found codified and established in a particular authoritative source, but that it is something that has developed over time and is continually being refined and developed.

Does this discussion help us with the example of the manager contemplating who to promote which we introduced early on? First, when the manager is wondering what to do, what is the guidance that comes from natural law? I think this is an easier question to ask than most – as I think most people would agree that one of the principles of natural law would be that we would not support discrimination, or the treatment of one group any differently than another (very much as Martin Luther King was arguing earlier). We should refuse to promote on the basis of personal loyalty – and accept the consequences of our actions if that becomes necessary – because that is not the basis on which the company operates. Of course, that is what we should do – as for answering the question as to whether this is what we would do, well that depends on whether or not we have the fortitude to do this, and put up with the complaints and hard feelings that might result. Not all of us are a resolute as Martin Luther King.

However, even in making the decision that there should be no discrimination, that the best qualified person should be offered the position, it turns out the situation is still tricky. Why? Because now we have to address a rather more complicated question: how do we define 'best qualified'? At issue here is not something as clear as which rules to apply – loyalty or impartiality – but the rather less easily resolved question of 'what are the criteria that tell you this is the best person for the position on offer'?

This takes us down an interesting path. Some areas of behaviour, and some rules, are clearly not just: while we may have some difficulty defining them, we can see and feel they are not moral, not part of that important package called natural law. In many legal systems that term 'natural law' is replaced by common law, the body of law that has developed over time, not just in the form of specific statutes, but also in terms of the arguments used to establish precedents. Some areas of law are far more contestable in the sense there is no clear principle that tells us that this is something we should be required to do. Of course, some people would argue that this applies to such things as paying income tax!

There is yet another issue to be considered here. What about when we are aware that someone else is breaking the law. What should we do then? Socrates would tell us that if we really want to understand something we should look at the 'big picture' first. So, it might be a good idea to take that advice, and consider the world of organisations and wrongdoing: here is a suitable big picture to consider. A telling example comes from looking at companies, and how a member of such an organisation responds to the situation where the company is doing something that does not appear to be legal or proper, or even just has some concerns. What do they do? Usually, a person with such a concern will go and tell their manager – and wait for the manager's advice. In many cases, the manager can salve their consciences by explaining what is happening – helping them re-examine the situation, sometimes showing that the concern was misplaced.

There are occasions, of course, where the manager invites their staff member to be complicit in allowing something to happen that should not. The appeal can be subtle "I am sure they know what they are doing", and sometimes it can be rather more blunt "I wouldn't poke your nose in there, if I were you". Maybe this same concerned person might decide to go further up the chain of command, and tell a more senior person. They may receive a good response. However, there will be some situations where a person has advised and appealed to the chief executive, and still not had their concerns resolved, and then decide to go 'public', and address the situation with an external body – an ombudsman, a regulatory agency. If the law is being broken and no one is listening internally to the problem, then some people decide to take the problem to those who are charged to act in such situations, or even decide to release a story to the media.

Such people, whistleblowers, really have to struggle hard: their moral conscience helps them push against organisational barriers and the disapproval of their colleagues. Are they rewarded for showing such determination? The evidence is that whistleblowers are almost always the people who suffer the most from making public comments based on their concerns. Certainly, a company can be punished as a result of a whistleblower's revelations. However, it seems almost to a fault, the whistleblowers suffer even more – often losing their jobs, and, curiously, their reputations. Why is this so? In many cultures the idea of 'telling on' your mates is seen as an ultimate sin. If you belong to a community (kids at school, members of a football team, part of the marketing division) what you don't do is tell someone else that someone has done something wrong. The schoolboy snitch is universally despised, 'sucking up to the teachers', not 'looking after his mates'. Is adherence to the community stronger than we might believe?

In a case we explored earlier, we considered the dilemmas of choosing the right person for a position. In looking at what the manager chose to do (to appoint on the basis of loyalty, or to appoint on the basis of future potential) you might choose to keep quiet about what happened, even though you considered his actions as using the wrong basis for making an appointment. Why would you keep quiet? It might be because you feared that the manager might seek to make your life uncomfortable as a result. Or perhaps you see yourself as facing the whistleblower's dilemma, preferring not to tell the authorities about something that has happened because to do so would be breaking a community rule – don't tell on others. Certainly the pressure to support your mates and not to tell is very strong. The situation of the whistleblower suggests that in practice loyalty is a strong ethic – a strong principle. Perhaps I could say a largely unquestioned ethic. We choose not to question the rule "don't tell on your mates", because to do so would be to suggest there might be principles more important than loyalty to the group.

The case of the whistleblower tells us that the rule of 'don't tell' is very strong even though the situation is clearly wrong, even where behaviour is illegal. What does this mean for those situations where the principles at stake are far more arguable? In our case study, where the manager is trying to decide whom to promote into his former position, suppose you are another member of staff observing what is happening. You may feel that the principles of 'fairness' are at stake here. One of the two people being considered has been a loyal worker for years – like you. Surely they should be given preference? Would you tell the manager that? If you did, you would probably be told it was "none of your business" (no-one likes being told what to do!). As to whether you would decide to go further up the organisation to raise your concerns – well, that seems very improbable to me. Even if you knew a more senior manager well, you would be unlikely to put yourself, and them, in the tricky situation of sitting in judgement on what criteria your manager should use. It is legitimately 'his business'.

Perhaps the comparison with the whistleblower is unfair. The whistleblower acted because something had already happened, or was continuing to happen, something serious. This was after the event. Suppose your manager makes a choice, and you feel it is blatantly unfair, because you are now looking at the action itself, from after the event. Would you then raise a concern? Perhaps you would do so obliquely, suggesting to some one at a more senior level "it was interesting that your manager had promoted someone on certain grounds?"

We looked at the case of the whistleblower because we wanted to understand what people do when they see someone else has broken the law. The big picture approach has led us to an interesting conclusion: there are strong pressures against bringing someone else's law breaking to the attention to the authorities. This seems to be because we treasure loyalty over bringing wrongdoers to justice. It appears that one cost of being in a group – whether it is a family, a group of friends, or an organisation – is that you have to live with the behaviour of everyone in that group. Is that always the case?

I remember when I faced a challenge on this issue. I was responsible for a membership organisation, and one of our members had been engaging in unethical practices, actions that bordered on being against the law. I was asked whether or not I was going to de-register him: kick him out of his membership, on the groups of unethical behaviour. After taking advice, I decided to leave the decision to someone else, in this case the legal system. What I decided to do was that I would de-register him if he were found guilty of illegal practices in court. To this day, I know that I backed away from doing the right thing, since his behaviour was clearly unethical, and he should have been thrown out. In fact, he managed to avoid ending up in court and remained in my organisation. Why did I back away? Was I unwilling to test the limits of loyalty versus good practice?

All this goes to confirm that in the world of organisations, we have accepted external control over our lives. We certainly are not 'in control': organisational rules are there to keep control over individual behaviour. Nor are we 'out of control', for we are being controlled. Surely that is true for most areas of our lives. We are neither wholly in control of what we do, nor are we free and out of control, but we are largely doing what is expected of us by society, by government, and by various agencies. This was what those early enlightenment philosophers were talking about when they addressed the idea of the 'social contract', the idea that we give up some elements of freedom in order to have the benefits of the protections offered by the state.

Today, there is a concern in some quarters that there is one form of control that is lacking: this is the mutual control that comes from spending time together with people in your community. This is not about rules and regulations, nor is it about habits and routines. It is about 'social capital', defined by Robert Putnam as those features of social organisation such as networks, norms, and social trust that facilitate coordination and cooperation for mutual benefit (see Putnam, 1993, for a fuller analysis). Is this about control, or is it about mutual understanding and trust, an element of relating with others that actually allows a degree of individual initiative? We might say that social capital does not prescribe behaviour, but provides a 'container' within which an individual acts with the understanding and support of those around them. Contemporary society, it is argued, has lost a lot of social capital, but relies instead on a more direct form of control through legal and regulatory devices.

Whether it is by mutual trust and understanding or by laws and regulations, to live in a community means that you are willing to sacrifice some level of freedom to be a member of the group. Glaucon suggested to Socrates that we do this unwillingly, because we would prefer to look after our own self-interest but we do not want to seen as breaking the law. However, there may be a different force at work here, which is our desire to belong to something, to affiliate with others. Rather than being against our human nature, this may be part of it.

We can see this clearly today. At one level, we all accept that living together means there are some general rules and laws you have to follow. However, at another level, we do not just live 'in the community': we seek out people with whom we share a common interest – in music, in paragliding, in reading the works of Thomas Mann. In order to link with these groups, we willingly give up some of our individuality, and follow some of the largely unwritten specific rules and procedures that each group has developed. Some of the time, we may find something irritating or unnecessary, and occasionally we choose to leave if we cannot either influence the group to change or if we cannot 'live with' that element of the group. We do all this with friends, too. Friendship also entails a willingness to set aside some of our individual preferences, and accepting our friends as they are, fitting in with their idiosyncrasies.

In today's digitally enabled society, there is another phenomenon emerging which makes this issue of 'belonging to a group' even more interesting. Many people today belong to virtual groups, established through the Internet, where members may live in far-flung corners of the globe. Here it is easier in some way to belong, because the absence of the 'whole person' means we are able to interact and accept the conventions of membership at a more superficial level. We do not know a lot about the others with whom we interact, and if we did, we might find membership more difficult!

Given that membership of any group or community means that we have to conform, that our behaviour is being 'controlled' to some extent or another, then is this always going to limit our capacity to make changes? What are we free to do? This was the concern that Mill addressed when he spoke about liberty, and argued that we should have complete freedom over our selves, our bodies and our thoughts – unless, of course, exercising those freedoms would lead us to limit the freedom of others. However, there is a different perspective on this, which is how you bring about social change, not just how you continue to exercise your personal freedom. This book is concerned to encourage you to examine your life, and think about the changes you would like to make. Given that living with others sees to require that we are willing to give up on some of the things we might prefer to do, we would not like to come to the view that the only certain way to change our lives is to live alone, outside of the community. To come to the conclusion that leading an examined life requires us to be hermits, well that does not seem to be a particularly attractive proposition.

Peter Singer, whose trenchant and unyielding logic we met earlier in this book, has been a strong advocate of making change, of 'pushing the peanut forward' as he once put it (Singer, 1993). In a way similar to Tawney talking about the importance of striving to achieve equality, Singer explains that we should continue to seek to change, to lead an ethical life:

> "None of this, however, is a reason for turning away from an ethical life in which we accept our own fallibility and do what we can, in immediate and practical ways, to make the world a better place. Voting for the right politician is not enough. When we put ethics first and politics second, we can judge people by what they are doing, now, rather than by who they vote for or what they would like to happen. Are you opposed to the present division of resources between the wealthy nations and the poor ones? If you are, and you live in one of the wealthy nations, what are you doing about it? How much of your own surplus income are you giving to one of the many organizations that are helping the poorest of the poor in the developing nations? Do you believe, perhaps, that there is no solution to world hunger without a solution to the problem of

our growing global population? Fine, but what support do you give to organizations that promote population control? Are you indifferent to forests being turned into woodchips? If not, are you recycling your waste paper? Are you against confining farm animals so that they cannot walk around, or stretch all their limbs? But do you support the agribusiness corporations that keep animals this way by buying the bacon and eggs that they produce? Living an ethical life is more than having the right attitudes and expressing the right opinions."

(Singer, 1993, p 225)

Perhaps this reminds you of our earlier discussion of Lao Tzu, and the importance of 'taking the first step'. Can we make changes in our lives that contribute to leading a good life? Of course we can, and while we may eventually aspire to make changes that reverberate through society, for most of us, it is the small steps, but steps actually taken, that matter.

The environmental movement has been a helpful example of how change can take place, small in each part, but having a major impact on society. Following concerns over the use of polluting chemicals and waste, people started advocating better environmental practice – recycling, composting, and buying products that had less environmental impact. Today I am staying in an apartment with five different waste bins – one for glass, one for paper, one for metal and plastic, one for organic waste, and one for anything that does not fit in the previous four categories. We have changed our thinking at an individual level about what we can do for the environment, and in so doing have helped companies think more about developing environmentally sensible products, as well as creating new business areas in waste and pollution management, energy production and so on. As we mentioned in an earlier chapter, all that began with a book about fish dying in a lake (Carson, 1962): the first of thousands of little steps taken, but cumulatively changing the world in which we live.

For each one of us, even though we may feel constrained in many areas of our lives, there are opportunities for us to take small steps. Peter Singer makes that very clear. The steps you take do not have to be as big as leaving your home and becoming a missionary, or an aid worker. That might not be the path you want to follow. That might not be the size of step you want to take now. However, that does not stop us looking at the changes we would like to make, and seeing progress as incremental, beginning with those things that are necessary and easy to change, and then letting the process unfold over time.

Can you change? Yes, you can, and this is the topic we will explore in the next chapter of this book.

Field Guide Criterion 8:
Expectation: Obedient versus Unconstrained

The criterion of 'expectation' is an important one, as it defines the degree of freedom that we have in our actions. In many ways, we live in a world where the expectation is that we will be obedient. Obedience is more than just following the law. It is about accepting the right of others, especially our superiors, to set down the ways in which we will behave. To challenge that right, even within the family, is a struggle. It is a struggle when we know we have moral clarity to aid us, when we know that an action is breaking the law, or that a regulation is unjust. It is a far greater struggle when the path to a better moral or ethical life is less clear, and where the choices to be made are more complex and contestable.

In this criterion in the field guide, we are exploring a continuum that runs from being in the world with no freedom of action to one where you are totally free to do as you wish. The first extreme, being totally obedient, is the world of automatons. The other extreme, being totally unconstrained, can lead you to the world of anarchy. As with all our continua, the challenge is to find the balancing point between these two extremes.

Once again, here are some questions for you to consider or discuss with others:

- How much of your life is taken up with doing what others tell you to do?
- What time do you set aside to reflect on what you are doing, and considering alternatives?
- On the other hand, how often do you question the rules that have been set, the way the world works, the ways people behave?
- Do you accept, or challenge?
- How easy is it for you to find a balancing point between these two extremes?
- Is that a comfortable place?

9
Opening our minds

At the beginning of this book we addressed our inability to see inside the minds (and views) of others, and hence the impossibility of really knowing how everyone else sees the world. This led us on to explore how far we believe we are like everyone else, how far there are differences, and from there to a discussion of human nature. However, there is another question that arises from that concern with knowing how others see the world, and that has to do with perspective – with our ability to see the world differently, to 'stand in another's shoes'.

In part this is about our willingness to spend time in reflection, in stepping away from doing things, and allowing ourselves to think about what has been taking place. There is a deeper level to this, where we go beyond mulling things over, and begin to examine how we make sense of the world around us, our 'taken for granted' frames of reference. John Berger gave a memorable account of these 'ways of seeing' in a book with the same name (1956) when he explored the frames of reference used by visual artists over the centuries and how they informed the art they produced.

Our frames of reference are deeply embedded, operating somewhere below our day-to-day thinking. Just as they first develop when we are young, so they can gradually change over time. In my late teens I was a typical middle class English young man; without really knowing it, I saw my world through the eyes of someone who was privileged, class aware but not class conscious, self-confident, somewhat paternalistic and expecting to be a leader of others (together with many other elements in that frame of reference I cannot so easily uncover now). I moved to Australia when I was 30 years old and within a few years slowly much of that had been replaced by another way of seeing the world - now I can recognise I see things through a different framework, more class conscious, less assertive about my own importance, and with a very different understanding of relationships between the sexes. Some of that change was going on beneath the surface. Some was more obvious, a reaction to the healthy Australian view 'Here comes another bloody Pom'! Perhaps some of that change would have happened wherever I lived; perhaps part was just from getting older in a changing world.

However, in this chapter, I am interested in another way in which these 'ways of seeing' can change. Instead of this happening naturally, over time, can we actually 're-think' how we see the world around us, and do so deliberately through some form of self-examination? How can we reveal the frames of reference that we use?

I was very fortunate in my education. After initially studying to be a geologist, I changed course at university, and became interested in social anthropology. That lead me to read the works of some wonderful researchers, who strove to help us see how the world looked through the eyes of people in very different societies. I can still remember the thrill of reading Malinowski's study of the Trobriand Islanders, Argonauts of the Western Pacific, (1957) and the way in which he managed to draw me into their lives. I learnt about the complications of families and kinship in another culture. I found out about the strange Kula Ring, a ritualised cycle of formal exchange between the chiefs of the Trobriand Islands and their neighbours: shell arm bands going one way around the cycle, shell necklaces the other. It was the first of many books where I had to grapple with trying to understand how others saw their environment and the people around them: a doubly difficult task, because they lived in a culture that was quite foreign to me, and I was yet to understand the extent to which I looked at things through my own embedded frame of reference. I found I had to replace an outsider's fascination – were young Trobriand women really as sexually promiscuous as Malinowski was saying? – with an appreciation of a different way to live. Young Trobriand women were not 'sexually promiscuous', they simply did not commit to a relationship quickly: those weren't his words, and Malinowski would have been horrified at how his description of growing up in the island had been understood.

Social anthropology was more than trying to understand the lived experience of others. Some studies were more technical, addressing theories to do with different types of kinship systems, or political arrangements. Some were about the intricacies of farming in environments that ranged from slash and burn forest locales in Africa through to the complications of the water regulated worlds of rice farming in Asia. Some were about the process of being an anthropologist. I remember with great clarity the shock of reading Levi Strauss's autobiographical account of his trying to be an anthropological fieldworker (in Tristes Tropiques, 1973), and discovering that much of the book was about him. That book revealed, possibly unintentionally, Levi Strauss's inability or unwillingness to immerse himself in the lives of another culture, remaining an outsider, comfortable at looking at things through the eyes of a French intellectual. It made me wonder if I had the ability to understand another culture, or if I too would be stuck in the worldview with which I felt comfortable.

Social anthropologists spend their time in the field learning the language, the culture, and the behaviours of another group, whose worldview and experiences are likely to be completely alien to their own. They then have the unenviable task of trying to convey all they have learnt and understood in words that we can read and understand. Inevitably, there is a degree of trickery in all this. It is relatively easy to explain the rules of marriage, the symbols of a ritual, or the rites of expiation before a primitive god. That does not help us understand how it is to the people concerned. Nor are we able to grasp the consequences of the willingness of their 'subjects' to help the anthropologist in his or her task. There are some wonderful photographs of Malinowski surrounded by Trobriand Islanders – he with his tent, pith helmet and tropical gear; they with their huts made from pandanus leaves, without hats and virtually naked. How did they perceive this strange apparition, and how did they construct their task in communicating with him. Was there any real connection, or did they tell 'stories' to give him some understanding, at a level they thought he would understand?

As good luck would have it, some 15 years after learning about the Trobriand Islanders, I had the opportunity to visit what was said to be still a largely unspoilt island, off the tourist track. Travelling in a small aeroplane, I found myself sitting next to a young man who turned out to be part of the Lepanu family, the family of the paramount chief. An old woman had died, and there was going to be a family burial and wake. He was an assured, well-educated young man, who would not have been out of place in government offices in Paris, or in the boardroom of a company in the USA. Yet he was able to throw off that cultural dress and become a Trobriander again.

Unfortunately, I wasted the opportunity to talk to him about his perceptions of being a Trobriand Islander while living part of his life in the modern world – I was too excited about the past, and spent my time asking about Malinowski, and how he was seen. Then, when the plane landed, I was confronted with a quite unanticipated problem of much greater significance. The European influence had made its mark in this formerly remote and idyllic island, and there it was, a cheap hotel for occasional tourists with native girls visiting you at night. The entrepreneurial owner explained that these were not prostitutes, but simply the beneficial consequence of the 'well known' sexual promiscuity of young Trobriand women (after all, he implied, wasn't this exactly what that anthropologist had documented?). The shock of that situation pushed out all thoughts about trying to understand how one could move seamlessly between living a traditional Trobriand life style and working and living in modern society. Instead, I fumed about exploitation.

Social anthropology was an invitation for me to learn about 'standing in another's shoes'. Today when I am talking to MBA students, I ask them to do exactly that. This is not because I want them to understand the culture of people living on a remote island, but more usually because I want them to think about such issues as how a customer sees their business, or how the sales people in the company see the engineers. Every time I do this, I wonder how effective that request can be. I remind my students that they are parents and consumers – does that help them see things differently? Sometimes, perhaps, but the act of changing your frame of reference when asked to, so challenging for the social anthropologists, is just as hard for us in our day to day lives. Indeed, in some ways it is harder: if you are an anthropologist in an alien culture, you know the world you are trying to come to grips with is likely to look very different from your own; if you are a manager in your own country, the effects of culture and frames of reference are just as pervasive, but possibly much harder to 'see'.

Stepping outside of your normal frame of reference requires that you accept that there are different ways of constructing the world, and that one perspective should not be given priority over others. This has been one of the central concerns in postmodernist analyses. These critics have sought to make it clear that we do not see things 'objectively' but rather make sense of things through embedded perspectives that imbue objects and events with meaning, through pervasive ideologies if you like. That postmodernist agenda has revealed how analyses and theories are often shaped and structured by a deep underlying narrative about how the world works, a frame of reference that is seldom explicit or clearly articulated. It seems it is not possible to see the world objectively. On the other hand, as Joyce Appleby and her colleagues observed, "Objects can be tough to abandon, for they exist" (Appleby et al, 2000). There are events that have taken place, physical evidence we can see, and their very existence puts a limit on the interpretations we can offer: we have to take account of those 'objects'. Moreover, the process of revising our views – and they use history as their example – does not mean that choices of perspective are arbitrary (the fear of relativists). Rather:

> *"Successive generations of scholars do not so much revise historical knowledge as they reinvest it with contemporary interest. Each generation's inquiries about the past actually carry forward the implications of its predecessors' learning. New versions of old narratives are not arbitrary exercise of historical imagination, but the consequence of the changing interest from cumulative social experience. If history did not involve a relationship with an object outside the self, it would have no capacity to extend the range of*

human understanding; its disclosures would only be reflections of ideas already known. The Dutch historian Peter Geyl commented that all history is an interim report, but he would not have denied that within those interim reports were residues of research that would be studied long after the interim of the report passed."

(Appleby et al, 1994, p 265-6)

Perhaps this is why I found social anthropology so interesting. In a world where there are so many possible ways of constructing the world, of how we see things, there are consistencies and structures that seem to keep on popping up. While I found the task of understanding the bases of narratives very hard – and still do – I now understand so much more. For example, I am more able to recognise male interpretations of the world, and have a better sense of the feminist interpretations of so much that I had taken for granted. Much of my behaviour has changed as a result, and their narratives have a core that I have been able to internalise.

Is it important to step outside those comfortable and taken for granted ways of seeing the world? Certainly, as part of an examined life, we might want to understand how clearly we shape the way we look at the world around us. We might want to go further, and change our perspective more consciously, more 'purposively'; we might want to deliberately rethink our frames of reference because we want to see things in a new light. This might remind you of that earlier discussion of Einstein's views about knowledge and Kuhn's discussion of scientific paradigms: we already have a way of making sense of things, and this makes the task of replacing it with another all the more difficult. However, while paradigms represent a coherent and explicit model of the way the world works, ways of seeing are less accessible to us than ideologies or paradigms: they are deeply embedded aspect of our culture and upbringing. We might know that we want to think differently, but there is no path laid out for us to follow. In the sense I am using the concept of 'reorienting', it is a tough task.

How can we help ourselves to see things in a new light? I am not suggesting that we should all seek to study academic social anthropology. However, at a more accessible level, travel offers us an opportunity to learn and reflect. In a sense this experience can be the basis of a form of practical social anthropology, observing and learning about other cultures as a way to help us see differences. I suspect that being in another country often means you spend time learning and reflecting on your own world, rather than seeking to understand another. Theodore Zeldin almost got it right when he concluded his chapter on travel by observing "A journey is successful when the traveller returns as an ambassador for the country he has visited, just as an actor is most successful when he enters into a character and discovers something of himself in the part he plays" (Zeldin, 1984). Actually, I think the analogy with an actor could have been taken further, and that a journey is successful when the traveller discovers something of himself in the act of understanding a culture that is not his own. When we look at people in another culture we also have the opportunity to see ourselves more clearly.

Imagine you are sitting in a bistro in a major city in the world, sipping coffee, and watching the world go by. As you do so, it is easy to begin thinking about the lives of the people who pass by. Sometimes, and often almost unnoticeably, you may find yourself thinking about yourself, what you are doing and where you are heading. Why is this? It is as if the same people who looked different, spoke another language, and who were foreign to you have now become like a set of mirrors focussed on you. You see yourself in difference and in similarity, and the process has the potential to explore and sharpen up that picture you have of yourself.

A more powerful opportunity for a deeper level of engagement comes through the discipline of learning another language. This might be at a basic level; enough to ensure you can talk to others and find your way around. Even more revealing, a demanding but rewarding task, is to become reasonably proficient so that you really communicate with others. When I travelled to other countries some years ago I used to be a tourist, looking at the sights and appreciating works of art, architecture, and the other visible evidence of another culture. Now I tend to stay longer in one place, try to talk to some people, and learn more about their lived experience. You find out so much more living in a small town, shopping, eating locally, and making some friends, than you can from being a visitor to a major city.

You have the opportunity to ask questions, and to probe into those things you cannot quite get right as you look around. When you have engaged in a real dialogue with people from a quite different part of the world, both you and they benefit: you both increase your understanding of each other, and yourselves. Those visits to sights and monuments do have a role to play, revealing the history and the influences on the people you meet. However, many real insights, and hence a renewed understanding of yourself, comes from that deeper immersion.

Somewhat removed from direct experience, I have also found books about the culture and life of another country helpful. Some are written by authors from my own cultural background, but sometimes they are the work of interested anthropologists, travel writers or cultural commentators whose own lives have been in very different cultures. Strangely, it sometimes seems that it doesn't matter if the story they tell is only partial or even biased. Rather, it is the way in which those stories reverberate against our sense of ourselves that matters. I don't know if all the stories in 64 Million Frenchmen Can't be Wrong are right (to quote one such title): I do know it made me think and reflect on many issues, only some of which were actually about France and the French. In reading that book, I began to think again about how I relate to other people, and about the way in which we look at our politicians (the French appear to be much more forgiving about the private lives of those in power, and just concerned that they get on and do what is needed for their country).

There are other ways in which we learn about how we make sense of our world. In conversations, people may make comments or observations that illuminate how they see us. These comments can help us identify our taken for granted framework: to be told I have an "English sense of humour" one day made me realise that I did have a particular way of making what I thought were witty comments (and helped me understand that not everyone else saw them in the same way!). However, listening is hard, as we tend to hear what we want to hear. We are good at filling in gaps. We are good at explaining to ourselves how someone has got things wrong. We are not so good at being open to really hearing another point of view, and absorbing why that person's perspective is different from our own. It takes a degree of humility that is often unfamiliar to us: after all, we do know ourselves and our place in the world better than anyone else!

The Greeks have a very good word to describe our inability to listen, because we are so confident about ourselves: it is 'hubris'. Sophocles wrote a play in ancient Greek times – Antigone. It is a powerful and rather frightening story, as it shows how King Creon cannot hear what his daughter, and later his son, has to say to him. In a way that anticipates the central theme of Shakespeare's King Lear, whose inability to really hear what others are saying to him is a path to tragedy. I cannot think of a better example of the importance of really paying attention to what another says, and the consequences of failing to do so. I have often thought that Antigone was mis-named, and it should have been called Creon. Antigone plays a key part in this drama and her actions create the basis of the story, but the play has as its centre Creon's hubris and his inability to reflect on the views of others, not Antigone's intransigency and moral certitude. Creon learnt to be humble far too late in the story.

Jim Collins wrote about humility in his book Good to Great (2001). In a study of a small number of successful companies, he discovered that his expectations about company leadership were incorrect. He assumed that the chief executives of such companies would be visionary, charismatic figures, motivational, engaging, and great communicators – the standard picture of the all-successful leader. In fact, all were a fascinating combination of two attributes: determination and humility, the determination to make their companies successful and the humility to be willing to always listen to ideas. They reminded me of Robert Greenleaf's description of 'servant leaders', people who are good at enabling others, articulating concerns and challenges, and clear about the outcomes that need to be achieved (Greenleaf, 1977).

I have found that teaching adult students can be a wonderful way to increase your humility. To be surrounded by a group of intelligent, thoughtful people coming diverse backgrounds and listen to their ideas, observations and suggestions, you quickly learn that you are one among equals, and everyone has things to contribute to a discussion. I marvel at the insights I get every time I explore some of the classical literature I have used in teaching over twenty years with a group of people: there is always a new perspective, a new reading of what is being said, and a new twist that I had never seen or considered. In any work environment we can always make good use of opportunities to hear the viewpoints of others if we are willing to listen, and be humble enough to realise that often they may have a more helpful perspective than yours.

Having lived in Australia, I have had the extra benefit of living in a high immigration country (similar to the USA, Canada or Israel). But that is putting too high a premium on the importance of ethnic diversity. People of different ages, genders or life experiences all have something to tell us, if only we will pay attention. To reiterate, that is to both to listen and then to hear what is being said.

Finally, we do benefit from the insights of others in other ways. The role of creativity and the arts in helping us see things in new light was explored in Chapter 6. Books provide a particularly powerful way to help us to see the world through another's eyes. Many books are factual, rewarding us through presenting us with the writer's findings, observations, their discovery of the intricacies of peoples' biographies or their explanation of the histories of other countries. Fiction, on the other hand, put us inside the frame of the writer's understanding of people, as we begin to live through the characters' experiences. After reading a really good book we see some things from a new angle, initially quite clearly so, and later, if we are lucky, that new perspective lingers on in more subtle ways. Reading a novel about a wine drinker who slowly moved from connoisseur to alcoholic eventually dying from cirrhosis of the liver has changed the way in which I have looked at wine ever since: not feeling that I should become a teetotaller, but as someone aware of his own potential to move beyond enjoying wine to becoming absorbed by it. We all face the risk of allowing enjoyment to slip into obsession.

We want to stand in another's shoes because we know there are different ways of experiencing the world and we can gain from understanding new perspectives. If we want to go further, to rethink our own way of seeing things, then that act of standing in another's place becomes all the more valuable. We may be able to understand more clearly the way we see things, and where change might be possible. We may be able to question why we prefer or tend to see things in the way we do, or go further and start to adopt a new way of seeing.

How do you adopt another way of being in the world? The answer to this question does not have to be to totally change your life and the way you live in an instant, like shedding a former skin, although that may be where you end up. It may be that you move down a path of change in small steps. Taking even a very small step in changing how we make sense of things may lead to realizing that you want to continue a process of change as you begin behaving rather differently. To give a simple example, I recovered a lost sense of enjoyment of food by spending time in France, and eating as the French do, sometimes with a group of French friends. I began to see food as more than just fuel, but as the experience of textures and tastes that are enjoyable in themselves: meals are not to be hurried, as an obstacle on the path to progress, but rewarding in themselves. The French seem to avoid eating while walking hurriedly around the city or while working. Eating a meal for them, it seems, is about creating a space, and a meal is an opportunity is to stop for a while. It might sound strange for someone with my background to say, but thank goodness for the French obsession with excellence in food!

Perhaps that may seem trivial. Twenty years ago, as the CEO of a small organisation, I was fortunate enough to take part in an Executive Seminar at The Aspen Institute. I was sent my book of readings – several of which have appeared in the extracts in this book – and then spent two weeks exploring and debating what these 'great thinkers' had said, and how their ideas applied to today's environment. At the time, it was a professional development program for me: by the time I returned to Australia, the seeds of change had been planted. I began to move back to my first love, teaching, and a few years later joined a university. The process has continued since then, affecting both how I teach and think, and the things I do: this book is yet another outcome of following a path begun with a small step many years ago.

So far this chapter has focussed to a large degree on understanding frames of reference, or ways of seeing, and doing so in order to rethink how we look at the world. There is another task, which is one path to gaining knowledge and insight, and this comes from reflection. There is a subtle but important difference between this and deliberately trying to rethink, where the task is focussed on changing our frame of reference. Reflection requires rather different approaches from those we have outlined so far.

Reflection is the process whereby we look back over things that have happened, experiences we have had, or plans we are developing, trying to sort things out, make sense, and understand better. It is a luxury that often it seems can only be experienced in solitude, or within a familiar environment where the mind is free to roam and explore. For some, that solitude can be experienced in listening to music, for others in sitting alone in a city square or park. I find that I need quiet to reflect, to experience real solitude, and therefore I seek places where there are no distractions – no contact with the busy working world, no telephone, computer, and no sense of others busily clamouring to be heard. In that silence I can slowly develop a train of thought, which is so easily lost when something obtrudes from the outside world.

On other occasions, as is the case while I have been writing this chapter, I find the soothing sound of familiar music provides a different kind of reflective space. Often familiar music can provide a background that blots out other sounds and interruptions: however, this can be a dangerous strategy for me, as there can be moments when the music breaks through, and I start listening – and the thread of reflection disappears from consciousness. In the same way, on yet other occasions, I like to talk with a group of people, pushing out ideas and thoughts, and listening to the views and responses those discussions create. Then I need to stand back again, and reflect on what has been said: sometimes I think I would like to be Gyges with that ring of his, able to talk for a while and then become invisible and think over what has been discussed!

What does this tell us about reflection? Reflection is when we stand apart from doing, and allow our minds to consider, analyse, and explore. Some reflection is for a clear purpose – at this moment in this chapter I am thinking about how I am going to express my ideas about rethinking and reflection. Some reflection is less structured, as when we mull over a topic, trying to make sense of something, or to find a way to deal with an issue. Either way reflection is time out from doing things busily or routinely. Time to reflect is precious, and in the normal working week, there is little opportunity to do so. One of the paradoxes of better living standards is that working people who might benefit from reflection seem to have little time to do so. On the other hand retired people often do have more time to reflect, and yet we find it hard to keep them engaged with workplaces and benefit from their observations and ideas. This is all the more strange in the sense that it was not all that long ago when the great majority of people died soon after retirement, never enjoying the opportunity to learn from reflection which they had so deserved.

Reflection is the way in which we acquire knowledge. On some occasions we need to reflect to ensure that we choose the better course of action. Typically at work or at home, you are invited to give advice on something, to make a decision, or to respond to a request: "I am going to hold a review with the team over that incident", or "Should I send this letter?" It is almost part of our nature that we tend to respond to such comments or requests immediately. It is hard to stand back and think about what is being proposed, and yet reflection before action so often pays dividends: yet we often justify our lack of reflection by believing there is no time to do so. Before agreeing to a review of an incident, it might be a good idea to try and understand what really happened. Instead of sending a letter, it might be better to review what you are trying to communicate to someone else, and how this might be done most effectively.

Today I encourage managers to make sure they ensure a little reflective time – even when they are under pressure. A few moments of careful thinking may allow you to come up with a far better response than the immediate answer you would otherwise provide. Ask a question, look for some paper to make some notes, just breathe in for a moment – but reflect! There is a skill in this. When I worked for an oil company many years ago, we used to emphasise the importance of 'helicopter', an ability which was described as being able to address an issue, and yet simultaneously stand back and see the issue in its broader context, and reflect on what was really at stake. We sought to identify this skill in staff, and even tried to train people in developing their helicopter ability. Alas, while the idea is hard to explain, it is even harder to realise in practice.

A very different experience of reflection is described by Malcolm X in his Autobiography of Malcolm X, (published in 1987, after his death in 1965). While undertaking the Hajj in Mecca, he felt the need to write some letters, and realised they had been developing in his mind for some time. He explains what happened:

> "..... on this pilgrimage, what I have seen, and experienced, has forced me to re-arrange much of my thought-patterns previously held, and to toss aside some of my previous conclusions. This was not too difficult for me. Despite my firm convictions, I have been always a man who tries to face facts, and to accept the reality of life as new experience and new knowledge unfolds it. I have always kept an open mind, which is necessary to the flexibility that must go hand in hand with every form of intelligent search for truth.
>
> "During the past eleven days here in the Muslim world, I have eaten from the same plate, drunk from the same glass, and slept in the same bed (or on the same rug) - while praying to the same God - with fellow Muslims, whose eyes were the bluest of blue whose hair was the blondest of blond, and whose skin was he whitest of white. And in the words and n the actions and in the deeds of the 'white' Muslims, I felt the same sincerity that I felt among the black African Muslims of Nigeria, Sudan, and Ghana."
>
> (Malcolm X, 1965, p 108)

That experience led Malcolm X to understand the importance of 'colour-blindness' in relationships, a perspective that because a key theme in his preaching. His thinking was developing in the context of undertaking rituals and talking with other pilgrims, a context that was quite different from that he experienced as a Muslim in the United States of America. For him, reflection was heightened through unfamiliarity, living differently, that helped him "re-arrange" his thinking. It was also not conscious in the sense that I described when I was thinking about this chapter: as Malcolm X was at the Hajj, so he was absorbing and considering ideas that suddenly crystallised and came together almost like a sudden flash of inspiration.

Can reflection be a source of inspiration, or even a form of revelation? Did Malcolm X open his mind to hear what he was being told? Perhaps this is a matter of words and their meaning. Revelation can be understood in religious terms as hearing the message of god; it can also be understood in a spiritual or intellectual sense, which is the kind of understanding what wisdom can bring. I see reflection as a path to greater wisdom; with greater wisdom, I may eventually be able to gain better insight into the sources of what little wisdom I have gained.

People tend to want answers to things, but I think that rethinking and reflection are not so much paths to answers, as ways to ensure you keep on asking questions. When Socrates used that phrase about an examined life, I do not think he was thinking about examination being like a test. Take the examination, and you will know the answers. Rather he was asking us to keep ourselves in touch with our lives, and saw the examined life as a lifelong task. For that reason, there is no answer as to how you should do this, no right way, as it were. How you ensure you keep rethinking and reflecting is a puzzle that only you can address – finding a way of living that works for you.

Field Guide Criterion 9:
Perspective: Reorientation versus Reflection

There is a tension between our capacity to rethink – to see things differently – and to reflect – to consider things as they are. In reflecting on ourselves, the difficulty is that it is easy to be comfortable, because we 'know the way things are'. To reflect is to re-examine what has been happening to us, to our relationships, to what we have been doing. It is a path to wisdom, but wisdom takes time because it is a level of thinking that is more than just knowing the way things are. Perhaps it is something on which we feel there is no need to invest much time.

At the same time, it is hard to reorient ourselves, to fundamentally change our perspective by stepping outside of our taken-for-granted way of seeing the world, and see things anew. Reorienting is very different from reflection. It has a purpose: demanding that we put aside one frame of reference, and replace it with another. That is a disturbing task, disturbing to our own sense of balance and equanimity, and disturbing to others because we now see and relate to them in a different manner: that change might be subtle, or it might be quite dramatic.

This last criterion in the field guide is about perspective, finding out where we are in terms of our vantage point on ourselves and others. The task of perspective is to find the appropriate balance between reflection and reorienting, between focussing on learning what we can about what has been taking place and adding to our stock of wisdom or focussing on changing our frame of reference and adopting a new perspective.

The final set of questions is to explore how you think about change:

- How do you refresh you perspective on the world, and on how you see and relate to others?
- How do you make sure you have time to reflect?

- What for you is the key balancing point between learning to see things differently as opposed to reflecting on what you have learnt?
- Why?
- Do you see this balance shifting in the future, and, if so, in what direction?

10

Now over to you

This final chapter is a summary of all we have explored – and a reminder of some of the questions you might like to address. Why a summary? I want to remind you that this is a field book, not a text to be read and then set aside: in reading this chapter, I want to encourage you to use this book in the way in which it was intended. Socrates was the starting point of this book, suggesting that "an unexamined life is not worth living". He did not tell us what the examined life was, but rather presented it as a practice, focussed on asking questions for yourself. This chapter is to remind you of what some of those questions might include.

It is interesting to note that Socrates did not tell us what made for a 'good life'. In fact, he was careful to avoid answering that question, since the question as to what constitutes a good life is an invitation to think about the personal and moral values you should adopt. Consistent with that approach, this book is intended to help you think about how to lead an examined life, but not provide a list of the specific values that should be important for you.

Why not list the values that underpin a good life? To receive a list of values is to step back from thinking and questioning, and to allow me (or someone else) to begin to provide answers for you. You already have a set of values, and, if you want to re-examine these, there are many sources available to help you explore and determine your values and consider which will be important for you in the future. Those sources range from religious texts and frameworks through to contemporary humanist rationalist visions. A re-examination of your values is part of the process of living an examined life, and the topics we have been exploring here should help you in that task.

At the same time, we have come to realise that values – or principles or laws for that matter – are often conflicting and incomplete. No one set of values in themselves provides the basis as to how we are to live, as they often contain contradictions and omissions which have to be addressed if we seek to put the ideals of values in to practice. The criteria we have explored in the previous nine chapters and the extremes that define them give us a basis for thinking about how we apply our values. At the same time, our analysis has suggested that using logic, and especially using practical reasoning, can help us see how to apply those values that matter to us in the face of the messiness of the world.

What are the values that are important for you? Perhaps you are a utilitarian, practical and pragmatic. Perhaps you are a believer in the golden rule, a guide to good living that is found in many books, religions and philosophies. Perhaps you are practicing Christian or Moslem. Perhaps you are a humanist, taking on Peter Singer's 'viewpoint of the universe', or just focussed on what makes us human.

Whatever the values we hold, they are the basis on which we make decision as to what is right or good, or what is wrong or bad. For much of the time, they are implicit and accepted. Many of our values were imprinted at a young age, by parents and school. In examining your life, you may want to go back and look at the influences that have shaped the values you have held to date, and think more deeply about how far they are consistent with your current views about the topics we have been discussing.

In this book we have examined nine topics:

- Making assumptions
- Ourselves and others
- Does economics make sense?
- Examining the world around us
- Reaching in to the future
- Acting strangely
- Theory and practice

- In control, out of control
- Opening our minds

Actually, I should confess I had a bit of fun in naming them, as the first letter of the ten chapters of the book, including this one, spell out the word 'moderation'! I am not sure if that is advice or a warning; moderation in all things leads to leading an unremarkable life – but without some degree of moderation, we can go to dangerous extremes! Perhaps we should quickly move on from this author's little game!

Each chapter, and the topics it explored, led us to uncover a number of criteria for you to consider – each one expressed as a continuum that is defined by an extreme at either end. I would like to list them slightly differently for our summary. Looking over those criteria, and the eighteen extremes that define them, it seems to me they fall into two groups:

- people as social beings (and includes 5 of the criteria), and
- people as thinkers (and includes the other four).

As social beings, we are constantly navigating between being part of a group; and carving out our own individual path. This group includes the criteria of:

Affiliation – (Chapter 1), with the extremes of individuality and community

Consideration – (Chapter 2), with the extremes of loyalty and impartiality

Allocation – (Chapter 3), defined by the extremes of equality and efficiency

Expression – (Chapter 6), with the extremes of conformity and creativity; and

Expectation – (Chapter 8), with the extremes of obedient and unconstrained.

As thinkers, we are constantly choosing between feeling confident and capable, single minded even; and being tentative and reflective. This group includes the criteria of:

Intention – (Chapter 4), with the extremes of pragmatic and theoretical

Organisation – (Chapter 5, with the extremes of confidence and uncertainty

Perception – (Chapter 7, with the extremes of ideological and open-minded; and

Perspective – (Chapter 9, with the extremes of reflection and re-orienting

Perhaps you will find this allocation of the criteria and their defining extremes too simplistic: I have found it helpful in my examination of my life, and in talking about these ideas with other people. I have used the framework to organise this summary – but you can just read each of the criteria without focusing on the two groups if you find that more helpful.

Group 1: People as social beings

We have identified five criteria that fall under this heading. They all have to do with the ways in which we interact with other people.

Affiliation - Community versus Individuality (Chapter 1)

As a social animal, we first have to balance between being part of a community, and being an individual. What does this mean? To be part of a community is to accept the 'social contract' we described earlier, to give up some of our freedoms in order to reap the benefits of belonging to a group. There is a lot of pressure on people today to think of themselves as individuals, and to expect to be treated as an individual, rather than members of a group. This may sound rather strange to you, as a lot of the time we talk about people in terms of their membership of a 'group' characterised by tending to behave in the same way: we see one person as a Roman Catholic, another as a banker, as this was an adequate picture of their character and behaviour. Sometimes we feel this goes even further, and begin to worry that the government sees as us numbers rather than as unique beings.

However, so much of marketing today is focussed on you, trying to persuade you that doing this will suit your distinctive needs and aspirations. While this is often so much 'hype', this approach is being extended today by a significant trend in manufacturing and service delivery. Companies around the world are trying to find ways to deliver their products and services to a customer of 'one', so that their service or product is developed uniquely, really done so on the basis of one person at a time. The cost of all that emphasis on you is that the people around you can become a less important part of your life.

We are all familiar with the situation that, despite our best intentions, we know few of the people living on our street: that the bonds of the local community may not be as strong as they were in the past. At the same time, we have partial membership of all sorts of other communities – through work, leisure and family networks (both face to face, and through the digital world). Why do I call these partial memberships? Because it is easy to sustain a 'distanced' relationship within many of these groups, only being part of that community for a specific purpose. For example, if you belong to a group of model railway enthusiasts, then you meet to talk about locomotives, insignias of the past, and devising various layouts and signals. However, when you meet, your relationship with your fellow enthusiasts tends to be limited and exclusive – the rest of you is left outside the door. The person who raises some other, personal matter is seen as showing 'bad form'.

Where do you sit on this community/individuality continuum today? Do you feel that your engagement with others is satisfying and rich, or do you feel that you are unable to be free as a person, that your individuality is under threat? If this was the first of the continuums we explored, it was for a good reason, as it is central to our experience as social beings.

Consideration - Loyalty versus Impartiality (Chapter 2)
The issue of consideration examines the way in which we relate to others. It ranges between the extremes of loyalty and impartiality, from accepting the claims of intimacy in determining our relationships, to living in an impersonal but fair world.

Intimacy in relationships is demanding, presuming that we will respond to all the elements of another person, not just dealing with one part of their character. Intimacy is about real engagement. It requires loyalty, respect and showing real care for another. It is the stuff of being wholly human, in a sense. It is also impossible. Clearly, we cannot relate to everyone we meet at an intimate level, and this was the dilemma about loyalty that we met in the second chapter of this book. To make life possible, we have to treat many of our interactions on an impersonal basis, fairly, impartially, applying the same rules in the same way. Yet that understanding is not always reciprocated: some people we treat fairly but impersonally expect us to respond to them loyally, personally, and do not want to be treated like everyone else. We are constantly being pulled from one extreme to the other, from loyalty to impartiality, often upsetting unintentionally whichever way we go.

Perhaps we need some rules to live by to make this area of our lives workable. I sometimes feel I have to be 'up front', and say to someone seeking my support that I will deal with this in the same way that I would deal with it were anyone else involved. I know that to treat people in such a manner is both brusque and denies their legitimate claim to be treated as an individual, but this approach is helpful, nonetheless.

Another way we can manage our relationships better is if we put some space in between receiving a request and responding: waiting for 24 hours may allow our stomachs to tell us what is right – or allow us to calm down from an initial reaction. This is one of the criteria for an examined life that I find very hard to manage, and I would not be surprised if the same was to be the case for you. Have you worked out how to manage this trade-off? Do you feel you have the balance right?

Allocation - Equality versus Efficiency (Chapter 3)
The third in this list of criteria that relate to us as social animals turns out to be one that is perhaps the most familiar. Discussions about equality versus efficiency have been part of the political discourse of many countries in the last 50 years, and seem likely to remain. In the same way, they are also built in to business operations, and inform the

ways in which businesspeople think and operate. I suspect that for many of us, the emphasis is towards the efficiency end of this continuum – is it for you? We are anxious to do things well, to use resources effectively, to reduce costs and to enjoy the benefits of success. We do recognise the importance of equality, and that everyone should have a chance to get on in life. At the same time, we are quite happy to use our network of friends to find a job for a child or a close friend, giving them an advantage not available to others. Many of us live accepting inequality, especially if we are fortunate enough to be living on the favourable side of the divide that inequality implies.

Are you comfortable with where you are on this continuum? Perhaps you are one of those fortunate people whose job and values are firmly directed towards ensuring equality; for you efficiency and effectiveness are merely measuring sticks to use to ensure the task is done in the best way possible. Perhaps you are one of those people who experiences that nagging feeling at times that you don't respect equality enough, that somewhere in the back of your mind you feel you should be doing more. This is often the motivation that leads many of us to work for not-for-profit organisations in one way or another: you may be a volunteer, or serve on a committee or a board. Is that enough? Just because this has become part of political debate, we are not excused from our individual obligation to think about this trade off, and be clear about what we see as the right balance to be achieved.

The notion of equality is a troublesome one: it is easy for us to see the differences between ourselves and others, and there is a continuing subtle reinforcement of the idea that we are unlike 'them'. Conceptually, we recognize that all people are the same: practically, we see difference all the time. Is difference a reason to deny equality? Do you feel conformable with how you see the people you meet? More to the point, do you see a common humanity with those who live in other countries, other places? Do you want to strike a different balance on this criterion?

Expression - Conformity versus Creativity (Chapter 6)

We do many things because of tradition; the way things have been done. This is exactly the kind of topic on which Socrates liked to question people. Why do you do this? He was never happy with the first answer, which was usually along the lines of 'that's what people do', and pursued each answer he was given with one 'why' after another. The opposite end of this continuum is creativity, having the ability – and the freedom – to do things that are new. I believe everyone is born creative, and it is only the weight of socialisation – at home, at school and then at work – that often suppresses those creative impulses. Just watch young children at play, and you will see a natural creativity that can be quite inspiring.

That is not to suggest that being conventional is a bad thing. At times it is comforting to follow routines, and not to stand out. It can be a balance against other sides of our life. As a person who often speaks in public, when I am at a party I like to disappear into a boring version of myself, conforming to expectations of others, wearing my tweed jacket and looking as though I am stuck somewhere in the early 20th Century! I am out of the limelight, and able to stop performing. I am sure many performing artists have the same desire to disappear into conventional behaviour much of the time: perhaps even Andy Warhol had his conservative and conventional side!

Perhaps, like me, there is a creative side to you that you have been unwilling to explore or allow to develop. In examining this part of our lives, the trade off is between having the time and freedom to do something new, and the sometimes overwhelming demands of conformity that work and family can bring. Every time I think about Socrates and an examined life, I think about 'space': space to think, space to explore, space to learn. Space to do things is at a premium today, as our lives are filled up with more and more 'stuff'. Or perhaps you are at the other end of this continuum, creative but doing so at the cost of avoiding the responsibilities that come with convention. To be creative can also be a selfish act, presuming on others to be a source of support and encouragement. Have you given some space to your creative side? If you have, is it at a cost to others? This is a tricky area in which to get the balance right.

Expectation - Obedient versus Unconstrained (Chapter 8)

Within the community and society more generally, the final continuum of importance in this group is that which runs from obedience to living without any constraints. Unlike some of the other criteria, both these extremes sometimes seem to have a negative connotation. To be obedient is to be seen as passive, subservient, as always yielding to the rules of others. To be unconstrained is to be someone who makes changes by breaking the rules and conventions. Such people are seen as irresponsible, dangerous even, pursuing their self-interests in a selfish way, not caring about the opinions or needs of others. Given these two extremes, there is a natural impulse here to find the middle ground, to be moderate. That must be a warning to us. Moderation is often a sign of unwillingness to consider alternatives, to change. The fact that the words are so value-laden is also a warning: obedience is really just another way of saying law abiding, surely a good thing. Someone who is unconstrained may just be a non-conformist, someone who likes to explore new ideas.

Perhaps we need to be both obedient and unconstrained: willing to follow rules and obligations where it makes good sense to do so, and be able to break free and do something new or change the rules when that makes sense. When we read about Martin Luther King earlier, he gave us a powerful example. You can support conformity and obedience when it is serving a good end, but you must consider being non-conforming, deliberately breaking the rules, when there are issues at stake that have a major impact on us and on our common humanity.

I wonder where you sit on this continuum today. I know that I have moved over the years, less willing to be constantly obedient, and more willing to stand up and argue for my values and concerns, even when this is something that does not fit with the current values or ways of behaving. Perhaps I have been lucky – in more senior positions, you often have the licence to practice some non-conformity, to be more radical in your approach. Perhaps this the effect of gaining some wisdom with age. Have you reached the point were obedience is stifling your ambitions? Or is it time you began to give way to some of the better rules and regulations that society has developed?

Group 2: People as thinkers

People are not just social beings; we are also thinkers. There are four criteria that seem to come under this second heading.

Intention - Pragmatic versus Theoretical (Chapter 4)

The first is probably the most challenging. I wonder if you are like me, and like to feel that you know what to do most of the time. I feel my skills are pretty good in most situations: one example is when I am preparing material to teach. I prepare some slides using PowerPoint, and do so using the same few techniques that I learnt many years ago. I am being practical, because I need to pass on some information. However, I tend not to step back and ask what I am trying to achieve, and how might this best be accomplished. Recently I was given a book about teaching and the preparation of materials, and in reading all that carefully collected theory realised I should rethink much of what I usually do. Why is it that we allow our beliefs about our pragmatic approach – and our technical skills – to roll over our need to gain better understanding? I wonder if you, like me, would love to gain more theoretical understanding – and even some wisdom. It seems to be hard to take the time to step back and ask questions about what we have learnt.

That was part of Socrates point, of course. An examined life means taking time out to gain understanding, and not just get on doing what we know. As with some of the other criteria, the trade off here is intimately involved with time: do we have time to take time out and think? Do you take time to think? Where are you on this continuum today, and would you gain from shifting in one direction of the other?

Organisation - Confidence versus uncertainty (Chapter 5)

If we are to change our lives, then planning for the future must be a key issue, and this is related to the next criterion on my list, which is the trade off between confidence and uncertainty. Confidence is about getting on and doing things, about applying practical skills and even practical thinking to the tasks we confront. We are comfortable doing what we know. We like to ignore ambiguity, the uncertainty of what is going to happen, the complexity of the things we try to address. There are enormous pressures on us to be certain, and to ignore the real indeterminacy of the world around us.

We live today in a particularly uncertain and volatile world. It is easy to deal with all that ambiguity by ignoring it, and go on with living in our own little space, insulating ourselves from the turmoil around us. We take comfort from being good at the things we do, and applying our skills to the tasks around us. Perhaps we should expose ourselves to some discomfort. I wonder if you would benefit from time out to think about the uncertainty and ambiguity that exists in your life, and how it is progressing. Or do always seeing the complexity and uncertainty, and not being confident enough to take action handicap you?

Perception - Open-Minded versus Ideological (Chapter 7)

I like to feel that I am very open-minded, always willing to listen to other points of view or learn from other approaches. I also like to feel that when I am addressing an issue, personal or not, I do so in a sensible fashion. Of course, I mislead myself. A lot of the time, there are unexamined ideologies and frameworks at work: my daughter asks me to do something, and I suspect that sometimes – almost without thinking – I respond to the request through the framework of a 'male' or even as a 'father': my daughter is an adult now, and is looking for the response of another adult, and a lot of the time I do not realise that I have not thought through either the issue or the relationship. In other words, our perceptions often contain within them embedded ideologies and frameworks: it is hard to stand back and sort out what is good advice, and what is merely the reflection of a set of views that we have adopted out of habit, without thinking.

To embrace a particular ideology is to take on a fairly coherent set of ideas and beliefs that guide our actions. The challenge is not about ideologies as such, it is about our willingness to subject them to examination, and to recognise how far they have inveigled their way into our day-to-day practice in an unconsidered fashion. Embedded ideologies can be very comforting, because they give us the reassurance that this is the way things are. Are you aware of the ideologies that inform your behaviour? Are you clear about how they influence the ways you relate to others? Are you willing to be more open-minded?

Perspective - Reflection versus Re-orienting (Chapter 9)

Not having enough time to do things is an issue that appears in many areas of our lives, and we explored this again in relation to reflection and reorienting, the extremes that define the last of our criteria, which I have called 'perspective'. Actually, this is an unusual criterion, in the sense that we tend to spend little time doing either of these. We do not have seem to have enough time for reflection, mulling over what has been happening, drawing together some threads of wisdom. It is almost seen as an indulgence, a time away from the things that we should be doing. Nor do we have time for re-orienting, the other more dangerous alternative on this continuum, where we deliberately seek to shift our frame of reference. This is not just about have making to think, it is about exploring how we might see things differently in the future, with a view to changing our perspective on how we are living in the world around us.

To say that we do not have time to reflect or reorient is a comment on our priorities. We make conscious choices all the time – 'let's "veg" and watch some television' – and many of those choices are deliberately not giving ourselves time to consider the importance of the issues on this continuum. Why is this? Are we uncomfortable about standing back for a while? To spend time on reflection or re-orienting is more than an indulgence, it is allowing ourselves to delve deep and to find out things that may be upsetting or challenging to ourselves, or to those around us. Are you ready to do that? To reflect or to re-orient ourselves is to take a decisive step on the path towards living an examined life.

A decisive step. That does remind me of Confucius, and the importance of taking the first step. In reviewing the list of criteria and beginning to examine each of the extremes, we are being invited to take some steps. My first step was going to a seminar – and I did not even realise how important that small step would prove to be: it was an invitation to start leading an examined life, and I did not even know it!

All I can do now is pass these ideas on to you, and invite you to continue the process.

Socrates thought an unexamined life was not a life worth living, and, of course, he was as demanding about this as he was with most of what he did. We do not live in Ancient Greece, with slaves to do the work and allow us to the luxury of almost unlimited time to think and to question. However, we can choose to devote some of our time to thinking about our lives, and what we want to do. Perhaps you have already taken that first step in reading this book. I hope you will take some more steps. Another might be to talk about some of these ideas with other people, and to delve further into the questions that they raise.

You are being invited to begin a journey, but one without any clear paths or milestones. It is a journey that may take place without your making lots of conscious choices about what to do next, but rather one that is driven by your natural curiosity. No clear signposts to suggest how you have progressed, and no defining characteristics which help you identify the next move, just a lot of criteria to accompany you as you travel. It may seem vague, but it is a journey worth undertaking. I want to wish you 'good luck' on your journey to an examined life.

Acknowledgements & References

There are so many people who have influenced me over time that it is hard to pick out just a few names. However, among those who have played a most important part are my teachers, especially Edmund Leach, who taught me how to read and think, and the basics of social anthropology; Charles van Doren, who introduced me to the Aspen approach: James O'Toole, who introduced me to the ideas of the good society; and the moderators at The Cranlana Programme, especially Jennifer Webb who reawakened my interest in an examined life. I started this book when I was living in Australia. It is a small country, and many of the leading intellectuals tend to wander overseas to be able to interact with a greater community of like-minded tinkers. However, it is people like John Carroll, Robert Manne and Peter Singer that keep our culture alive and question our comfortable assumptions. I owe them a debt and I hope they continue to flourish and be a source of provocative comment.

Apart from these, there are a host of writers whose books and articles have been a constant source of stimulation. I have provided a list of a few of these that you might want to read first – but once you get on to individual writers, it is easy to find their books. However, I would mention Project Gutenberg (www.gutenberg.com), a wonderful repository of out of copyright great books. Finally, there is a list of references quoted in the text.

Here are some overviews you might like to read to start your reading:
Allen, J S, 1983, The romance of commerce and culture, Chicago: University of Chicago press
Ciulla, J. B., 2000, The working life, New York: Times

Denby, D, 1996, Great books: my adventures with Homer, Rousseau, Woolf, and other indestructible writers of the western world, New York: Simon and Schuster

O'Toole J, 1993, The Executive Compass: business and the good society, Oxford: University Press

Van Doren, C, 1991, *A History of Knowledge*, New York: Bird Lane Press

There are many more to be found, and I am sure you find them.

References:

Appleby, J, Hunt, L and Jacob M, 1994, Telling the truth about history, New York: Norton

The Aspen Institute, 1997, The Executive Seminar: The Aspen Institute Readings, Volumes I and II, Aspen: The Aspen Institute

Bentham, J., Mill, J S, and Ryan, A, 1987, Utilitarianism and other essays, Harmondsworth: Penguin (reprint edition)

Berger, J, 1956, Ways of Seeing, Harmondsworth: Penguin Books

Carroll, J, 1993, Humanism: the Wreck of Western Culture, London: Harper

Carson, R, 1962, The Silent Spring, New York: Houghton Mifflin

Carter, S L, 1997, Integrity, New York: Harper

Collins, J, 2001, Good to Great, New York: Harper and Collins

Confucius, The Analects (see below)

Davies, P, 1995, About Time, London: Viking

Fletcher, G, 1993, Loyalty: an essay on the morality of relationships, Oxford: Oxford University Press

Friedman, M, 1962, Capitalism and freedom, Chicago: University of Chicago Press

Gilbert, K, 1989, The Blackside, Harmonsdworth: Penguin Books

Greenleaf, R K, 1977, Servant leadership, New York: Paulist Press

Hagel, J III, Brown J S and Davison L, 2010, The power of pull, New York: Basic Books

Handy, C, 1990, What is a company for? President's Address, Royal Society for the Arts, London; reprinted in Handy C., 1995, Beyond certainty, London: Hutchinson

Heifetz, R, 1994, Leadership without easy answers, Cambridge, Mass: Harvard University Press

Heifetz, R and Laurie, D L, 2001, The Work of Leadership, Harvard Business Review, December
Hobbes, T, Leviathan (see below)
Hyman, S, 1975, The Aspen Idea, Norman, Oklahoma: University of Oklahoma Press
Johari, J C, 1987, Contemporary Political Theory, New York: Advent
King, M L, 1963, Letter from Birmingham City Jail, published in King's book in 1964, Why We Can't Wait, New York: Harper and Row
Kuhn, T, 1962, The structure of scientific revolutions, Chicago: Chicago University Press
Lao Tzu, The Tao Te Ching (see below)
Levi-Strauss, C, 1973, Tristes Tropiques, London: Cape
Lightman, A, 2011, "The accidental universe", Harper's Magazine, December 2011
Locke, J, Two treatises on government (see below)
Luft, J and Ingham, H, 1955, "The Johari window, a graphic model of interpersonal awareness". Proceedings of the western training laboratory in group development
Machiavelli, N, The Prince (see below)
Malcolm X, 1985, Autobiography of Malcolm X, (as told to Arthur Haley) New York: Grove Press
Malinowski, B, 1922, Argonauts of the Western Pacific, republished by Dutton, New York, 1953
Marx, K and Engels, F, 1848, The Communist Manifesto, (see below)
Merriam Webster, 2010,
<http://www.merriam-webster.com/dictionary/machiavellian>
(accessed 10/9/10)
Mill, J S, 1859, On Liberty (see below)
Okun, A, 1970, The political economy of prosperity, Washington: Brookings
O'Neill, J, 1993, The Paradox of Success, New York: Putnam
O'Toole J, 1993, The Executive Compass: business and the good society, Oxford: University Press
Plato, The Republic (see below)
Popper, K, 1959, The logic of scientific discovery, London: Routledge

Powers, W, 2010, Hamlet's Blackberry, New York: Harper
Prahalad, C K, 2004, The bottom of the pyramid, New York: Pearson Prentice Hall
Putnam, R, 1999, Bowling alone, New York: Putnam
Rada, J., 2009, The Kitty Genovese Murder American History @ Suite 101
Rawls, J., 1971, A Theory of Justice, Cambridge: Harvard University Press
Rawls, J, 1999, Collected Papers, Cambridge: Harvard University Press
Schumacher, E F, 1973, Small is beautiful, New York: Harper and Row
Schwartz, P, 1988, The art of the long view, Sydney: Prospect, for the Australian Business Network
Sen, A, 2009, The Idea of Justice, London: Penguin
Shell, 2010, Scenarios <www.shell.com/scenarios>
Singer, P, 1996, Rethinking Life and Death: the collapse of our traditional ethics, London: St Martins Griffin
Singer, P, 1993, How are we to live? East Melbourne: Text
Sternberg, E, 1994, Just Business, London: Warner
Stoves in India, New York Times, April 16, 2009
Tawney, R H, 1952, Equality, London: Capricorn Books
Thomson Reuters, 2010, Intelligence, Intuition and Information, July 2010 - <http://thomsonreuters.com/content/corporate/PDF/Intelligence_Intuition_and_Information.pdf> released July, and accessed on 1 August 2010
Thucydides, The Peloponnesian War (see below)
Whyte, W H, 1956, The organisation man, Harmondsworth: Penguin
Zeldin, T, 1984, An Intimate History of Humanity, New York: Harper Collins

Quotations from the cited works of Confucius, Hobbes, Lao Tzu, Locke, Machiavelli, Marx and Engels, Mill, Plato, and Thucydides are taken from the digital versions of their works at Project Gutenberg, www.gutenberg.org. Other short quotes have been included on the basis of fair use for educational purposes. Permission for the longer quotes from Peter Singer were given by Random House, Australia. I was unable to find the current holder of copyright for the poem by Kevin Gilbert: if you know who that is, please let me know.

www.ingramcontent.com/pod-product-compliance
Lightning Source LLC
LaVergne TN
LVHW011417080426
835512LV00005B/111